ESCAPE

From Controlled Custody

Tony Lesce

Loompanics Unlimited
Port Townsend, Washington

This book is sold for informational purposes only. The publisher will not be held accountable for the use or misuse of the information contained in this book.

ESCAPE FROM CONTROLLED CUSTODY
© 1990 by Tony Lesce
Printed in USA

Published by:
Loompanics Unlimited
PO Box 1197
Port Townsend, WA 98368

Cover and Illustrations by Kevin Martin

ISBN 1-55950-038-7
Library of Congress
  Catalog Card Number 90-061242

Contents

Introduction

Escape from captivity is one of the most fascinating subjects of all time. This is because the yearning for freedom is deeply seated in our personalities. Gaining freedom from a political tyranny is rarely as interesting as escaping from physical captivity. Many people who have lived under tyranny all of their lives don't even know that they're oppressed. Most of us submit to some form of petty tyranny at various times in our lives, anyway, and survive. However, it's impossible to be confined to a cell or a barbed-wire compound without being acutely aware of it and thinking of escaping.

From the moment the first jail or prison camp was occupied, inmates started thinking about ways to escape. In many cases, the means were simple, because the systems of captivity were uncomplicated. Running away from a labor gang while the guard's distracted is a very simple, but effective, way of gaining freedom. The top-of-the-line prisons, on the other hand, are tough nuts to crack.

"They have their exits," as one British officer stated with regard to leaving a maximum security prison camp without the owners' permission. Devising means of escape from a foreign prison is a test of intellect, as well as emotional stamina.

People are continually devising more intricate and efficient means of keeping others captive. Prisons now have closed-circuit TV, electronic alarms, and other security systems, all aimed at keeping the inmates inside. It requires more ingenuity to break out or to sneak out.

This book will deal with both military and civilian prisoners. Military POWs are subject to different rules in most cases. In some locales, no rules apply except those of the occupying power. Civilians, usually convicted of violating a section of the criminal code, have no internationally recognized rights.

This isn't just a book of escape stories. It's also a practical handbook of escape techniques. The purpose is to provide the reader with a solid framework of knowledge to use in escaping from a military POW camp or from a tyrannical regime.

Some approaches to escape and evasion are inspirational. They claim that the will to survive is the most important factor. While it's true that morale is very important, knowledge of tactics is equally vital. More to the point, you can't obtain will and morale by reading a book, no matter how inspirational the text may be. These have to come from within yourself. Anyone who promises you otherwise is trying to sell you snake oil.

What you can pick up from a book is techniques and tactics for overcoming practical problems. You can learn tactical building-blocks, which you can later adapt to the situation you face.

Part I lays out the apparatus of confinement and repression, showing how a prison system works. We'll study barbed wire and walls, electric fences and prison cells, and the human system that runs the prison. We'll take a good look at the mentality of the guards, the problems in recruiting competent guards and coping with turnover.

We'll also study the methods prison administrators use to keep their charges docile. Besides walls and deadly force, captors use psychological methods, attempting to demoralize the prisoners. Intelligence gathering is a common aim, and prison administrators use informers to keep a finger on the pulse of the prison, and to discover escape plans before they can bear fruit.

Part II deals with techniques of escape and evasion. This will lay out step-by-step the methods prisoners have used to nullify security systems. This section will explore techniques of exploiting the weaknesses in any prison system, and how to make the most of each weakness discovered.

Part III describes some of the great escapes of the Twentieth Century. This section will show how determined men took advantage of their captors' laxness and laziness to carry out some of the most daring escapes in recorded history. The Twentieth Century is the perfect timeframe for selecting escape stories, because this century has seen the most effective prison systems and the most monstrous tyrannies to infest the globe, and the people who broke free used great ingenuity and showed outstanding emotional stamina.

Part IV presents a summary of practical advice for anyone ever taken prisoner.

Part I

1

Prison Systems

Prisons serve different purposes, in both the civilian and military categories. In civilian life, there are short-term holding facilities, usually known as "jails." These consist of cells and perhaps a "day room." Long-term incarceration is in "penitentiaries," or what we normally call "prisons." These have more elaborate physical plants, including workshops, classrooms, and other facilities for "rehabilitation." In states with capital punishment, prisons have "death rows" and execution chambers. Overlaying everything about a criminal prison is the heavy mantle of punishment. Although many inmates claim that they were confined as a result of an imperfect system of criminal justice, or even framed maliciously, they're confined because of a real or alleged misdeed.

By contrast, prisoner of war camps are made for men (and sometimes women) who were captured fighting for their country, an honorable enterprise. The German greeting to POWs: "For you, the war is over," reflects the good-humored outlook. Although some cultures, as we'll see, consider capture dishonorable, there still isn't the same stigma as there is to being a criminal.

Military prisons can be "stockades," designed for disciplining one's own offenders, and various sorts of camps for housing enemy or other personnel. The regular POW camp is usually a set of barracks sur-rounded by gun towers and barbed wire. In the best sense of the term, the POW camp is a "human warehouse." The servicemen confined have committed no crime, and are just in "cold storage" until the end of the war. There are also special punishment camps run by the military or by a para-military organization. Some of these are labor camps. Others are death camps, designed to kill the inmates. All can be very unpleasant.

There are also differences in confinement philosophy. Some prisons depend on bars, walls, and fences to keep people in. Others are "gun prisons," in which the main restraint against escape is the threat of be-ing shot during the attempt. Prisons in American Southern states tend to operate in this manner. Prisoners working in "road gangs" and "chain gangs" have only the guards' firepower between them and free-dom.

Cultural Clashes

Apart from the differences in interests between the captors and captives, there are also other factors which can make the prisoners' lives unhappy, and even tenuous. In World War I, there were no fundamental differences in outlook between French, British, and German views of prisoners of war. In World War II, there were notable differences, partly because of the greater number of belligerents, and partly because of changes in thinking. On the German side, there was a vast difference between the treatment given British and French POWs, and that reserved for the Slavic POWs, whom the Nazis regarded as "subhuman." Another difference was in the type of camps reserved for various classes of captives. Military POWs from the Western Allies got relatively good treatment in camps run by the German armed forces. Only 4% of British, American, Aus-tralian, and New Zealand soldiers in German POW camps died in captivity.[1]

Guerrillas, such as "Maquis" and "Partizaners," were not protected by international law. These often wound up in death camps after a brisk interrogation by the Gestapo. Members of ethnic groups the

Nazis considered inferior, such as Jews and Gypsies, were headed for extermination camps from the start.

The standard of living of the captor nation also counted for a lot. Even when strictly following the Geneva Convention and providing POWs with the same rations served to one's own troops, there were often large-scale dislocations. Italian Army rations were poor by British and American standards, and though Italians tried very hard to be humane, POWs in their hands suffered. Asian soldiers subsist on a few bowls of rice a day, which Europeans found inadequate. When the captor power is a subsistence economy, its captives can expect little. This isn't calculated cruelty, but simply the result of economics.

In Asia, standards were vastly different overall. The Japanese who took American and British servicemen prisoners during WWII followed the code of "Bushido," which considers surrender dishonorable. According to the code, surrender by a Japanese soldier was punishable by death. A Japanese soldier who had been taken prisoner, whatever the circumstances, had to make up for it, and in August, 1944, over 1,000 Japanese POWs at Cowra, Australia, stormed the fence armed with clubs and other improvised weapons for just this purpose. The Australian guards used gunfire to repel the Japanese, and shot 231 of them dead on the spot. Still, 334 of them broke out, fanning out in the surrounding countryside. They were quickly rounded up, either captured or killed.[2]

Japanese, imbued with this attitude, viewed the Allied servicemen whom they had captured as scum, unworthy of decent treatment. This is why they conducted such horrors as the various "death marches."[3]

Treatment varied, depending on the situation and the personnel. Front-line Japanese soldiers seemed to have had a more understanding and humane attitude towards their prisoners than rear-areas soldiers who did not see combat. The "combat men" did not impose any unnecessary hardships, but the farther to the rear prisoners got, the more they experienced the calculated rigors of Japanese hospitality.[4] Overall, 28% of the Anglo-American POWs taken by the Japanese died in captivity.[5]

In Vietnam, Americans captured were mainly airmen shot down over North Vietnam. The North Vietnamese saw them as war criminals because of the extended bombing of civilian targets in Vietnam. There was an intense effort to obtain "confessions," both for propaganda and as reprisals against the prisoners. In certain instances, there were deliberate tortures, such as tying a prisoner up into a ball.[6] Another torture used on airmen who refused to talk was having their arms tied behind their backs, and being pulled up by the wrists until the arms became dislocated at the shoulders.[7]

In primitive countries, prisoners of war can expect little in medical care. Their captors simply don't have the means to treat disease and/or injuries according to Western standards.

Political Conditions

Strongly affecting the way prisoners are treated is their political state, and the context in which they were captured and imprisoned. Criminals, of course, are seen as evil-doers paying for their crimes. Uniformed servicemen are, theoretically, protected by one of the Geneva Conventions. It's important to note that not all nations have signed one of the Conventions (there were several, in 1864, 1868, 1906, 1929, and 1949), and not all of them accept all of the principles completely.

In certain cases, the captor considers even uniformed servicemen as "war criminals." If there's been an atrocity, the captor will probably stage a public trial and sentence those found guilty to extra penalties, even death. Adolf Hitler ordered summary execution for the Red Army's political commissars, on the grounds that they were not legitimate fighting men but "political indoctrinators."

If the POWs are not members of regular armed forces, their captors probably will treat them like criminals. This is for several reasons, both legal and practical. One is that the Geneva Conventions cover only members of the armed forces, not "rebels" and "partisans." The 1949 Convention deals only with prisoners taken in a declared war. Another is that the established government, in case of a rebellion, does not want to ascribe any legitimacy to the rebels, and recognizing them as legitimate troops would be affording them a status that the government doesn't want them to have. The various Geneva Conventions dealt only with uniformed soldiers, and not civilians or guerrillas. Although the rebels might proclaim themselves to be "freedom fighters," it's simpler to treat them as bandits, because it gives security police officers greater latitude for interrogation. Criminals have no rights under international law; only the rights allowed by the national government.

We've seen this happen frequently during the last couple of decades among the Western nations. The British do not recognize the Irish Republican Army and treat captives as criminals. Likewise, Italy treats its "Brigata Rosso" as bandits. Germany sees the "Red Army Faction" in the same light as its predecessor, the "Baader-Meinhof" gang, as criminals. In the United States, members of the "Symbionese" and other "liberation armies" were not given POW status.

Another practical point is the relative strengths of the two sides. If two approximately equal nations are fighting, anyone holding POWs has to consider the possibilities of reprisals against one's own captured servicemen, and retribution after the war. If a national government is fighting rebels who do not hold any POWs themselves, there's little to fear, unless the insurgents win.

Local conditions can be critically important. If one side is very short of supplies, or is encircled and has no room to house POWs, they're likely to be executed after a quick cigarette. One of the unpublicized events of WWII was the verbal order circulated among American troops at Anzio, ordering that no prisoners be taken. Any Germans who surrendered were given a last cigarette, then taken "out back" and shot.[8]

Wearing the enemy's uniform is forbidden by international law. There have been many soldiers captured while doing this being court-martialed or even shot out of hand. Spies, and members of various secret service organizations aren't covered. An escaping POW, if he's wearing civilian clothing, can expect treatment given to a civilian or spy.

Guerrillas are not covered, and any civilian who fights against the other side's armed forces can expect to be treated like a criminal. So can a mercenary, except where he's fighting as part of the other side's legally established armed forces. The "soldier of fortune" can normally expect a "terrorist" label, and summary execution or perhaps a show trial. Members of para-military groups also get summary treatment, although they may view themselves as legitimate fighting men. Francis Gary Powers, pilot of the U-2 shot down over Russia in 1960, never got recognition of his military status, and stood trial as a civilian. Several American fliers shot down over Red China while on reconnaissance missions during the Korean War were treated as spies.[9]

Finally, an important point is who wins the war. The winner can put the loser's leaders on trial for "war crimes," while simultaneously violating international law. Soviet Russia, for example, did not release the last of its German POWs until 1949.[10] In the end, of the Germans taken prisoner by the Soviets, 50% died while in captivity.[11] Allied powers in the West used German POWs for clearing mine-fields around the end of the war.[12]

Initial Treatment and Classification

In both criminal prisons and POW camps, the administrations classify and separate their charges at the outset. In criminal prisons, the administrators seek to separate the hard-core recidivists from the younger prisoners who may be susceptible to their influence. They also assess their inmates according to security risks. Obviously, condemned prisoners and "lifers" are slated for maximum security. Those with mild sentences, who have much to lose from an escape attempt, are more likely to find themselves trustees or to go into work-release programs.

In POW camps, one of the first efforts is to separate the officers from the enlisted men. This is partly to break the chain of command and discipline, and partly a carry-over from the old European class system. Even today, for example, officers are not, in principle, expected to perform physical work, while enlisted men may find themselves in road or harvest gangs. POW camp administrators also are concerned with security risks, and those whom they consider likely to try to escape go into maximum security camps. The most famous such camp in WWII was "Oflag IVC" (Offiziers Lager) at Colditz, in Germany.[13]

Another serious concern for the captors was extracting military information from their prisoners. In this respect, officers were generally in better positions to obtain valuable information than enlisted men, and captured officers got most of the attention from interrogators.

As a start, both sides subjected prisoners to ruses. One was the "Red Cross" form, which had spaces for name, rank, and serial number, but also unit designation, home base, and other information of military value.[14]

Those whom the camp administration assessed as having valuable information wound up before skilled interrogators. There were several approaches which the interrogators took. Few, if any, involved violence. There was, however, other pressure, such as very uncomfortable cells which, the interrogator assured the prisoner, was only a temporary accommodation, as the prisoner would soon be moved to a much more comfortable camp after the formalities were over. Physical pressure would also come in being made to stand for hours, sometimes naked. In other cases, prisoners did not get to go to the bathroom for many hours, and some had to urinate in their pants.[15] Things were quite different among the Eastern nations. The Japanese, for example, used bamboo skewers under the fingernails to persuade prisoners to talk.

Allied captives in Germany, and German captives in Britain, were the subjects of various sophisticated low-key tactics to gain information. One would be the tea and cigarette approach, with an informal chat about home and family. This would inevitably lead to more important topics. Another was by suggesting that the prisoner, if he had parachuted into occupied territory, might be a spy or saboteur instead of an airman. Of course, answering a few "routine questions" would clear up the matter.

Another trick was the "stool pigeon," a turncoat prisoner who would start a conversation and feed whatever information came out to his captors. Not all camp administrators used stool pigeons. A microphone in a double-occupancy cell would pick up conversations, although there was no way to direct the conversation into an interesting channel.

Interrogations on both sides of WWII were exercises in guile. Interrogators would often be members of the same service, but on the opposite side. Luftwaffe officers would interrogate RAF captives, because they knew the tasks and the needs, and had the specialized knowledge that a police officer, for example, would lack. In some cases, interrogators would, if they spoke the other's language well enough, impersonate prisoners' countrymen.

Korea and Vietnam did not follow the pattern. There were beatings, and tortures of various kinds. One was being forced to kneel on jagged stones. Another was being tied so that the prisoner had to remain on tip-toe to avoid being strangled by a noose around his neck.[16] The more "civilized" Western nations also tended to use torture more since WWII. The civil wars in Algeria, Malaya, Kenya, Cyprus, and Aden, produced accounts of rigorous interrogations. The Israelis and Brazilians have also used torture to extract information from guerrillas and partisans. The war in Northern Ireland has seen British security forces torturing members of the "Irish Republican Army" to whom they don't accord the rights given to soldiers.

It's easy to see that there's no general rule for treatment of POWs, just as treatment accorded to civilian and criminal offenders varies widely. POW camps operated by the Germans and housing British and American servicemen during WWII were country clubs compared to Asian camps during and after WWII.

Sources

1. *Prisoners of War,* Ronald H. Bailey, Chicago, IL, Time-Life Books, 1981, p. 13.

2. *Ibid.,* p. 15.

3. *Prisoners of War,* A. J. Barker, NY, Universe Books, 1975, p. 122.

4. Related to the author by a veteran of Bataan death march.

5. *Prisoners of War,* Bailey, p. 13.

6. *Prisoners of War,* A. J. Barker, p. 3.

7. *The Raid,* Benjamin F. Schemmer, NY, Avon Books, 1976, p. 11.

8. Related to the author by a veteran of the Anzio landing.

9. *Prisoners of War,* A. J. Barker, p. 24.

10. *Ibid.,* p. 185.

11. *Prisoners of War,* Ronald H. Bailey, p. 13.

12. *Prisoners of War,* A. J. Barker, p. 112.

13. *Ibid.,* p. 125.

14. *Ibid.,* p. 61.

15. *Ibid.,* pp. 68-69.

16. *Ibid.,* p. 71.

2

Physical Security

Prisons are not necessarily in isolated areas. A prison or POW camp laid out in a remote location soon brings with it housing for the guards' families, and a civilian economy to support the prison. Residents of established communities often object to having a prison built next door, but the merchants prosper from the increased trade.

Physical Facilities

Prisoners need housing and camp administrators need security. Housing is in cellblocks in criminal prisons, and barracks in POW camps. Cellblocks contain individual or double-occupancy cells to keep inmates separated. Barracks are usually platoon-size.

In criminal prisons, high walls usually separate the inmates from the outside world. Military camps depend more upon barbed wire, plowed strips, and patrols. The main reason for the difference is that criminal prisons are permanent. Indeed, many have been standing for a century or more. Military camps are active only for the duration of the war, and any great capital expenditures would be wasteful.

A serious error is to try to adapt an existing facility as a prison. The design may be unsuitable, and require many expensive renovations before it's adaptable as a prison. A more serious problem is existing construction features which may defeat security. There may be old drains, for example, which are blocked off and invisible to the guards. However, the prisoners, with much time on their hands, will be seeking out features such as this to exploit. If a drain leads to the outside, it's a ready-made tunnel, and requires only access to it from inside the prisoners' quarters. Smaller holes and cavities in the buildings can conceal escape gear. Despite the obvious drawbacks and problems, governments make this mistake again with each war.

Another problem comes from having any area accessible to the prisoners adjoining offices or guard quarters. If prisoners can gain entry to an unguarded area by breaking through a wall or crawling through a false ceiling, this offers a ready-made escape route. There were many such design features exploited by the POWs at old German castles such as Spangenburg or Colditz. These were supposed to be maximum-security POW prisons, but they had many more escapes than the Germans anticipated.

Prisoners of war exploited a serious error in the design of Stalag IIIE, at Kirchhain. The west wall of Number 4 Barrack faced directly out onto a disused rifle range behind the camp, and this was practically an invitation to breach the wall to gain freedom. POWs immediately started scraping away at the mortar holding the cement blocks together. Late one evening the work was complete, and the escapers pushed the loosened blocks out onto the rifle range. Twelve escapers went through the hole.[1] Oflag XXIB, at Schubin, was a converted girls' school, and had many features that degraded security. Because this camp had not been originally designed as a prison, there were many blind spots between the buildings. The camp was built in rolling country, with cover provided by the terrain and the many trees. The perimeter wire was only seventy feet from some of the barracks, making tunnels easier to dig. The soil had good drainage, another feature in favor of tunnelers.

In both criminal and military prisons, a double wall or fence with sally-ports is a desirable design feature. The fencing is a double row of barbed wire, which may in rare cases be electrified. Coils of barbed wire can occupy the space between the two fences. An extra security feature is a low fence or rail, several yards inside the inner wire, setting off a warning zone. The guards warned the prisoners that crossing the rail and approaching the wire would result in being shot without further warning.[2]

If guard towers are directly above the wire, there are blind spots between two guard towers where prisoners can sit or lie next to the fence and remain unseen because seen from that angle, there are no gaps between the fence posts. This is why it's desirable to have extended platforms on the guard towers. These allow viewing straight up and down the sides of the walls and fences.

Very few camps have electrified wire. The power drain, if the current is truly lethal, is too high for a war economy. Maintenance of an electrified fence is expensive and difficult, because any breakdown in the conductors or insulators puts the fence out of action.

If the fence is electrified, the most economical way to use it is to announce the fact to the prisoners and to keep the power on only a few hours a day, not telling them when the fence is turned on. The deterrent value of the fence is the same, whether or not the power is on 24 hours a day. A minority of prisoners are irrationally afraid of electricity, and won't approach the fence at all if they think it might be "hot." Those who are not deterred will find means to insulate themselves while they cut the wire, and it doesn't matter if the power is on or off around the clock.

The purpose of the sally-port (Figure 1 on page 20) is to create an "air-lock," with only one gate open at a time. This allows guards to scrutinize and examine closely anyone or anything entering or leaving. It also blocks any attempt to "rush" the gate.

Towers on both sides of the entrance allow an overview by guards. If there are weapons in the towers, access should be only through a locked door, to prevent prisoners' rushing the tower and capturing the weapons. Depending on the threat posed by the prisoners, there may be full-auto weapons to quell any riot or assault by prisoners.

A system of patrols, observation towers, and even electronic sensors secure the perimeter of the prison or camp. There may be closed-circuit TV, heat and motion sensors, microphones and ground tremor detectors, and other sophisticated devices to economize on manpower.

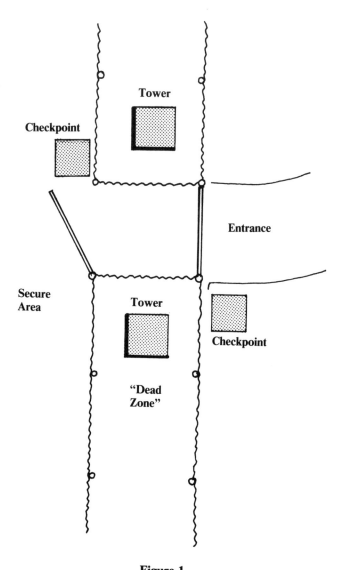

Figure 1

*A sally-port is a double gate mechanism
which adds security while discouraging escapes.*

A system of keeping guards awake at their posts during long and quiet shifts is essential. Sleeping guards cause serious gaps in security. At the New Mexico State Penitentiary, there were two escapes in two years under the noses of sleeping tower guards.[3]

Physical facilities range from very old and solidly-built to very new and flimsy. No prison, however, is any better than the system used to retain the prisoners. The security system usually proves to be the more challenging task.

Sources

1. *Escape From Germany,* Aidan Crawley, NY, Simon and Schuster, 1956, pp. 120-121.
2. *Ibid.,* p. 15.
3. *The Hate Factory,* W. G. Strong, Agoura, CA, Paisano Publications, 1982, p. 21.

3

Security Systems

It's true that "stone walls do not a prison make," but Richard Lovelace, the poet who wrote that line, had no real idea of the complexity of modern security systems that make a prison almost escape-proof. The most important components are indeed the security systems, including personnel and administration. All prison systems face the same problems, but solve them in somewhat different ways.

Personnel

Prisons and prison camps the world over have the same problem: they have to make do with second-rate human material in recruiting their staffs. Civilian prisons operate with low budgets, and correctional officers are poorly-paid, compared to police officers, and other civilian occupations. Prison guards are usually people who can't make it in the civilian economy, and who prefer the security of a civil service position to frying hamburgers or operating gasoline pumps. An unfortunate fact is that this type of job attracts coercive personalities, people who tend to be bullies.

Military prisons for POWs don't use elite troops as guards. Typically, they use reservists who are over-age or physically unfit for front-line duty. Because they assign personnel to guard duty instead of seeking volunteers, there are fewer problem personalities among the guard staff. Coercive types and sadists may occasionally find their way in, but they're far scarcer than among civilian guards.

Overall, POW camps have a higher grade of staff. This is because the guards are second-rate only in the sense of being unfit for front-line duty, not because they're necessarily "losers" in the civilian economy. Another reason is that the POW camps are always "ad hoc" organizations, brought into existence upon the outbreak of war. There are no POW camps in peacetime, and no opportunity for corruption to become entrenched as it does in criminal prisons. Yet another reason is the high caliber of prisoners. POW camps hold well-trained and well-motivated men under military discipline, compared to the odd lots of sociopaths confined in criminal prisons. They're far less likely to try to corrupt the guards and co-opt them into smuggling drugs, although they may corrupt them into smuggling food or letters.

Training for civilian guards is often poor. Although many prison systems make a pretense of training, with an in-house "academy," this is often minimal training and mainly concerned with the proper way to write reports or apply for sick leave.

Military guards get better training, partly because they're part of a military force, and partly because the national government somehow always finds the resources to train military personnel to do their jobs.

There are often morale problems among the guards, but this is more common in civilian prisons than in POW camps. Poor pay often lowers morale. Civilian prison guards often perceive that the administration is like a feudal domain, with a few top administrators more concerned with their personal benefit than running the prison or the guards' welfare. They also see that some of them are required to work in unsafe conditions, exposed to attack by prisoners. Another point which degrades morale is the well-publicized policy that a guard's life is, ultimately, expendable. Prison wardens cannot surrender to extortion by prisoners who take hostages, and make it clear that under no circumstances will they open the gates to a hostage-taker. The policy also includes the warden's life, but he's usually not the one taken hostage because he rarely ventures among the prisoners. In certain instances, such as the Attica uprising of 1971, guards taken hostage may even be killed by security forces recapturing the prison.[1]

Intelligence and Security

Because prevention is better than coping with a problem after it's begun, prison officials seek to inform themselves about events and trends inside the walls or wire. Each prison administration has an "intelligence" and/or "security" officer. This person often occupies a slot immediately under the commandant or warden. His task is to ferret out important information about escape attempts and to oversee security measures.

Routine Security Measures

The intelligence or security officer also directs the routine activities, such as patrols and searches. A program of routine patrols around the outside of the perimeter is essential if there are any escape detection techniques employed, such as plowed strips outside the wire. In many prisons, there are two walls or fences, and the strip between them is barred to all but security personnel. Keeping this strip freshly plowed discloses any attempt to cross it. Using patrol dogs to seek out escape efforts requires regular patrols by dogs and handlers. In POW camps, dogs are simply patrol dogs, and there's no need to employ "nark" dogs or dogs trained to detect explosives. In criminal prisons, narcotics dogs are very helpful, and often save many man-hours of searching.

In both criminal prisons and POW camps there are frequent head counts. These are to keep track of the prisoners, but also have a disciplinary function in keeping prisoners used to obeying orders by the guards. The repeated exercise of authority in calling the morning roll-call, or "appel," reminds the prisoners who is really in charge.

There can easily be as many as four appels per day. Guards taking prisoners to an outside work detail will count them before leaving the walls and count them upon arrival at the work site. They'll count them before starting back and upon their return. There are also general counts. Guards will line up the inmates and count them, or count them in their cells. If the count comes up short, they then have a general identification parade, in which each person's identity is verified and checked off against a list of inmates. This can take hours, because guards check each prisoner off against an identity card with his photograph and, sometimes, his fingerprints.

There have been enough escapes set up with dummies taking the place of the inmate in bed that some prison administrations have changed the cell count procedure. They now require all inmates to stand up and grip the bars of their cells while being counted. In some cases, prisoners are required to state their names to the passing guards. This avoids the possibility of fooling a guard with a dummy.

Contraband

In criminal prisons, the administration declares more items contraband than in POW camps. Part of the reason is punishment, and another part is control. Possession of ordinary items cannot be taken for granted by a prisoner in a criminal prison. The administration makes it a "privilege" which it can grant or revoke, depending on the inmate's attitude or cooperation.

Mail censorship is part of prison security in both POW camps and criminal prisons. Prison administrators are concerned about escape attempts planned by mail, but there are other concerns. Pornography is contraband in some criminal prisons. The definition of pornography depends upon the whim of the administration, and news-stand magazines are often forbidden. Military administrators scan outgoing mail for military information, as well as coded messages.

Modern POW camp administrators know of the code systems used to allow POWs to communicate with their governments. They don't have the personnel to scan every card and letter. A simpler solution is to restrict mail severely. In Vietnam, the Communist captors stopped most mail, and in 1970 most of the mail was hand-carried by Cora Weiss, co-chairman of the Committee of Liaison with Families of Servicemen Detained in North Vietnam.[2]

In both types of institutions weapons are contraband. However, in POW camps, there are few improvised weapons. A zip gun or "shiv" simply won't impress a professional soldier, who knows that it takes more than crude weapons to defeat even the guard force's armament. By contrast, a criminal will go to great lengths to make a home-made weapon. A toothbrush, when sharpened, serves as a "shank." So does a hacksaw blade or other small tool. Criminal inmates manufacture zip guns from pipe, using match-heads as propellant and nuts and bolts, even small stones, as projectiles.[3] These can be deadly at very close range, and are serviceable for prison assassinations.

Inmates of criminal prisons have regular visits by friends, relatives, and attorneys. Visits can be under very strict control. In maximum security prisons, visitors don't come into contact with inmates, but face them through thick armored windows and speak through telephones. Medium and minimum security prisons have visiting rooms, and even allow prisoners to walk in a fenced area with their visitors. Visitors who enter the prison pass through electronic gates to ensure that they're not bringing in weapons. In many prisons, visitors are allowed in only after background checks. An inmate who wants a certain person to visit him must submit his name and address, and the prospective visitor must fill out a questionnaire. Only visitors on the "approved" list are allowed in.

After the visit is over, inmates leave by one door, and visitors by another. This is a potential security breach, and only the distinctive prison garb prevents an inmate from walking out with the visitors. The visits are closely supervised to prevent a visitor's exchanging clothing with an inmate.

Inmates who are serving time for minor offenses or who have little time left on their sentences may even get passes to spend the day outside the prison with their visitors. However, all inmates undergo strip searches after visits, to ensure that they're not bringing in any contraband. This often includes a rectal examination.

Periodic searches of prisoners' quarters and belongings is an essential security measure. In civilian prisons, there's always the danger of contraband's being smuggled in by visitors and, to a lesser extent, corrupt guards. In both criminal prisons and POW camps prisoners can obtain contraband from home through the mails, by bringing it in on their persons, and by improvising it. POWs, however, don't get visits by friends and relatives, so for them this avenue of smuggling does not exist.

In criminal prisons, relatives and friends often bring radios, televisions, and other items for their inmates. Prison guards never let these straight into the inmates' hands. They first go to a special office where guards inspect them, and disassemble them as far as necessary, to assure that no contraband is hidden within. Packages arriving through the mail also don't go to the prisoners, but get similar treatment.

In many cases, POWs bring escape materials in with them. One example is the shirt or coat button that conceals a tiny compass. This is part of an escape and evasion kit issued to aircrews.

The Red Cross supplies parcels to military prisoners. These always contain food, and may also contain clothing, books, and other materials. The Red Cross supplies parcels in "bulk," not addressed to specific individuals. These typically arrive in carload lots. Packages from relatives are, of course, individually addressed.

POWs consider canned food as important escape gear. This is because they use it for sustenance if they make it outside the wire. Prison administrators consider this contraband, and often puncture every can sent in via Red Cross parcels to prevent prisoners' stockpiling food. Another measure is to ration out food parcels, instead of handing the entire shipment over to the prisoners at once. This is also to avoid stockpiling escape supplies.

POW camp security officers scrutinize parcels arriving for prisoners very carefully. This can pay off, as an incident during WWII showed. A German censor noticed that books arriving for British POWs had covers that seemed unusually thick. They all came from a source in Lisbon that turned out to be a front for the British Secret Service section set up to organize escapes. The thick covers contained hidden compartments with German currency, maps of German frontier areas printed on silk, hacksaw blades, and compasses. The prison security officer remembered that other parcels of books had arrived from this source, and started back-tracking. He confiscated some books from the prisoners' library, and found more contraband inside them. He also collected similar books from individual prisoners, but their secret compartments were empty.[4]

In POW camps, there were also roving patrols that walked around the camp looking for unusual activity and sometimes descended upon the prisoners' quarters unannounced to conduct searches. These were called "ferrets," and they would seek out tunnel entrances, stocks of escape gear, and other illicit activities. Some would crawl under barracks floors to search for escape tunnel entrances. They would also tap walls, listening for hollow sounds, and would inspect any place that appeared suspicious. They'd look for fresh dirt in the cracks between floor-boards, and under the barracks. They'd also look for fresh dirt on the ground anywhere in the compound, as a tip-off that there was digging going on.[5]

An advanced technique used by some ferrets was to construct hidden observation posts in the woods surrounding a camp and to observe the camp from there, using optical instruments. This gave a fresh point of view which sometimes would help disclose escape activities.[6]

There were often official visitors inside the compound. These might be Red Cross officials, electricians, and other workmen. After several escapes through impersonation of an official visitor, camp security officers devised the system of numbered passes. Every person visiting the prisoners' compound received a numbered pass upon entering. This might be a cardboard tag or a brass disc. The visitor had to surrender the pass when leaving, as well as show his papers. This system allowed a more accurate logging in and out of visitors, and helped avoid situations in which more people left than entered.

Informers

Every criminal prison has its network of "snitches." An intelligence officer doesn't have to try very hard to recruit these, because inmates are constantly seeking opportunities to secure advantages for themselves, and many are willing to betray fellow prisoners to get privileges or "time off." There truly is "no honor among thieves."

Informing is a dangerous occupation. In criminal prisons, snitches face reprisals if discovered. Their victims are eager to settle the score when "payback time" arrives. In a riot, snitches face death and mutilation.[7]

It's much harder for a security or intelligence officer to build up a network of informers in a POW camp. The inmates are generally fit young men, with military training and subject to military discipline. It's standard practice for the military chain of command to remain intact in a POW camp, and inmates are under control by their senior officers. Betrayal to the camp administration is treason, and this is, theoretically, punishable by death.

Still, it happens. In some cases, if the stool pigeon is not particularly dangerous, the prisoners will tolerate him, accepting him casually.[8] In other situations, reprisals can be severe.

There was a court-martial of an alleged informer held by German POWs in Cultybraggan Camp, in Britain, in 1944. Sergeant Wolfgang Rosterg had been charged with giving information that frustrated an escape by other prisoners. The verdict was "guilty" and he was executed. However, the British did not see this as a legitimate court-martial, and tried six of the prisoners involved.[9]

There was also a case of a Polish officer POW informing on his fellow prisoners in Germany during WWII. He was court-martialed but not executed. It was not until the American experiences in Korea and Vietnam, however, that large-scale betrayal became common among POWs. For reasons beyond the scope of this discussion, American servicemen were easy to turn against their fellows, and there were many noted cases of Americans currying favor from their Communist captors by informing on other prisoners or signing "confessions" in return for better treatment. That this was mainly an American phenomenon was highlighted by the experiences of the Turks, who also fought in Korea and who also had men captured. None of them informed or betrayed their country in any way, as far as is known.

Countering Escape Attempts

Security officers varied in competence, but the best of them were clever, subtle, and above all, patient. This showed itself best when frustrating escapes by tunnel. Almost every POW camp had one or more tunnels in the planning stage, actually digging, or complete at one time or other. Security officers instructed the guards to seek out signs of tunneling. Some of them are:

- Fresh dirt strewn around the courtyard.
- Unusual traffic by prisoners to and from a specific barrack.
- Dirt on prisoner's hand and clothing.
- Gradual disappearance of bed slats.

An eye for small details is important. One escape attempt from a British criminal prison, Parkhurst, fell through because an alert officer noticed that an inmate had mud on his boots.[10]

Security officers also used buried microphones to detect the sounds of digging. This had at least two effects. One was detection of digging in progress. If the guards were open about the emplacement of the microphones, it would force the tunnel diggers to dig their shafts more deeply to avoid detection. This made it more difficult and time-consuming.

Once guards detected a tunnel, they would, if they were subtle, allow the prisoners to continue to dig in the belief that they had not been detected. Upon completion, they would station guards at the tunnel exit to scoop up the prisoners as they emerged.

Good security officers knew that it was far better to let prisoners continue with an activity that they were already monitoring, instead of stopping them cold and having to ferret out the next attempt from scratch.[11]

Destroying tunnels, once found, was not as easy as it might have seemed. One way was to send someone down the shaft to pull the shoring and allow the tunnel to collapse, but this was dangerous. Another way was to pump in water, which would often do the same thing. If the tunnel's construction was especially solid, blasting was the only way.

Weapons Policies

Weapons are as much a part of a prison or prison camp as they are part of the police or armed forces. It's traditional policy to use gunfire to stop escapes or to suppress riots or assaults by prisoners. For this reason, POW camps and maximum security prisons are likely to have full-auto weapons mounted on towers overlooking both the prison yard and the surrounding fields. The threat from these weapons is usually enough deterrent, and examples of needing full-auto fire to restore order in a prison are extremely rare.

Long experience has brought about one well-known rule, not always followed strictly: "No weapons inside the walls." This is because desperate convicts have occasionally snatched the weapons and turned them on the guards. The rule applies, of course, mainly to firearms, and guards may walk within reach of the prisoners armed with clubs, saps, stun guns, or chemical sprays. Only guards in enclosed galleries, on the walls, or in the towers normally carry firearms.

There have also been attempts by prisoners to secure hostages, sometimes using home-made weapons. All prison staff are alert to this, and understand that, if they're taken hostage, their lives are expendable. There are some security measures to help alleviate this problem. Prisons have shooting policies and signals. At one well-known state prison, tower guards watch very carefully over any staff members who enter the yard, and keep alert for a shooting signal, which is a non-verbal request for "fire support." If a staff member points his finger at an inmate, then drops his arm suddenly, the nearest guard will shoot that person.[12]

There are also contingency plans to cope with riots, escapes, and other emergencies. Prison administrations can call upon the state police for help, and if the difficulty is beyond them, the National Guard. Commandants of POW camps call upon the nearest armed forces base for reinforcements.

Control and Discipline

In most criminal and military prisons, inmates wear uniforms. Criminal prisons issue uniforms, which sometimes are highly visible, with stripes and even bright targets on the front and back to use as aiming points.

The main feature of prison life, both criminal and military, is regimentation. Reveille is at a fixed time each morning, as are meals and other activities. Prisoners have to line up for inspections, roll-calls, sick call, meals, etc., and guards spend much of their effort enforcing the routine. The prison routine is administratively simpler than any other system for running a POW camp, and in criminal prisons the mind-deadening monotony is part of the punishment.

Further prisoner control is by restricting movement inside the prison. There may be a system of passes needed to go from cellblocks to work areas, recreational areas, and other facilities. Travel to the infirmary or visiting area usually requires a pass.

To maintain control and enhance security, there's usually a curfew at night. In criminal prisons, inmates are locked into their cells. In POW camps, the curfew requires all prisoners to be inside their barracks after the announced time. The barrack doors are not necessarily locked, but anyone caught outside is subject to arrest and punishment, or to being shot.

Criminal prisons use "privileges" as part of the discipline. Upon admission, the prisoner is told forcefully that he has absolutely no rights, and that he has to "earn" privileges by obeying orders and by good behavior. This system uses rewards for behavior modification. In the more rigorous prisons, there's an effort to break down the individual's personality and produce conformism.

Outside work details vary with the prison and the prison system. There may be escorts for work details. Near the end of WWII, there was a particularly nasty outside work detail devised for German POWs in Holland. German prisoners were used to clear mine fields. This resulted in 210 POWs killed, and 460 wounded.[13] Whatever the system, it's certain that some prisoners will be studying it carefully, looking for the gaps and weak points. If they act upon their observations, this will reveal if the system's as good as the planners had thought.

Sources

1. *A Time To Die,* Tom Wicker, NY, Quadrangle Books, 1975, pp. 269-298.

2. *The Raid,* Benjamin F. Schemmer, NY, Avon Books, 1976, p. 30.

3. *A Time To Die,* p. 88.

4. *Colditz, The Full Story,* P. R. Reid, NY, St. Martin's Press, 1984, pp. 131-132.

5. *Escape From Germany,* Aidan Crawley, NY, Simon and Schuster, 1956, p. 37.

6. *Ibid.,* p. 35.

7. *The Hate Factory,* W. G. Strong, Agoura, CA, Paisano Publications, 1982, pp. 65-79. This is a graphic account of how, during the 1980 riot, inmates entered the cells of the known snitches and tortured them to death. In some cases, snitches faced castration. Others were killed with acetylene torches or clubbed to death.

8. *They Have Their Exits,* Airey Neave, London, Coronet Books, 1953, p. 33.

9. *Prisoners of War,* A. J. Barker, NY, Universe Books, 1975, p. 124.

10. *The Master Book of Escapes,* Donald McCormick, NY, Franklin Watts, Inc., 1975, p. 137.

11. *Ibid.,* pp. 111-113.

12. Related to the author by prison official.

13. *Prisoners of War,* A. J. Barker, p. 163.

4

The Human Factor

Prison is an artificial environment which puts unusual stress on the human personality. The confinement, discipline, separation from home and family, and often the uncertainty of release combine to make prison almost unbearable. For some, it *is* unbearable.

Mental Illness in Prison

It's hard to generalize about this, because we can't say that confinement causes all cases of mental illness found within the walls or wire. Some "mental cases" are that way before arriving, especially in criminal prisons. POW camps have their quotas of battle fatigue cases. The only certainty is that treatment, if any, is inadequate.

The proportion of mental cases varies. The prison psychologist at one well-known prison in the Western United States estimated that, of his 1600 inmates, 300 of them were psychotic. There was no psychiatrist assigned to the prison at the time, and the only "treatment" the psychotics could expect was a prescription for a tranquilizer from the prison physician.

An important factor in helping prisoners keep on an even keel was news from home. The Geneva Convention specifies that POWs may exchange letters with friends and family at home. It's also customary to allow this in criminal prisons. In both, this "privilege" is sometimes interrupted for disciplinary purposes. In Korea and Vietnam, Allied prisoners often never got mail from home, and often were not allowed to write home.

News from home was so important that POWs took chances to obtain and maintain clandestine radios. Some of these were smuggled from camp to camp to allow POWs to hear the BBC broadcasts.[1]

Sex in Prison

This is the forbidden topic, but it exists. The sex drive does not shut off when the gates close. Except in camps that starve their prisoners, the sex drive exists. Authorities differ regarding how prevalent homosexuality is in prison. Some say that it's widespread. Others say that less than the majority become involved.[2]

Criminal prisons permitting conjugal visits, sex between inmates and their spouses or sweethearts, are rare. POW camps, because they're in foreign countries, cannot arrange this at all. This contributes to tensions within the prison camps.

Some inmates become openly homosexual. Others are forced into it by older, tougher convicts. In some cases, fights break out between older "daddies" over rights to a "punk." These can be lethal encounters.

In POW camps, there are similar situations, but they're either more low-key or the violence is better covered up. Under military discipline, there's less likely to be a sexual free-for-all. Another important factor is that POWs are not the dregs of society, but high-spirited young men who represent the best their country can turn out.

There are special situations, but few become documented. One that did, long after some of the participants were dead, was the allegation of a homosexual relationship in Colditz, the German POW camp.[3]

Entries in the diary of the British chaplain allude to a homosexual liaison between some of the British officers. One former prisoner, asked to comment on it, stoutly denied that any such incident had occurred or could occur. This is hard to believe, given the long term of imprisonment and that a couple of hundred British officers were involved. The British officer class tended to come from British "public" schools, which have the reputation of being hotbeds of homosexuality and other perverted practices. It's hard to believe that none of their graduates would have carried over his schoolboy sodomy into adult life, especially in this all-male environment. One more likely explanation is that these events occurred during the 1940s, between people brought up in an earlier era, when this topic was one that "polite society" simply didn't discuss. Today, with a more open attitude towards sex, it's easier to admit that healthy young males confined for years without women are likely to develop another form of sexual release.

Personal Clashes

The prisoner's organization in POW camps is usually very solid. However, there are occasional factions and these can be very serious. In Colditz, the German maximum-security POW camp, French officers at one point felt that the Jewish officers among them had betrayed an escape tunnel to the Germans. They requested that the Jews have separate facilities from those of the Gentile officers.[4]

Later, in Korea and Vietnam, the captors actively exploited personality conflicts between prisoners, and strove to create differences in order to keep the prisoners divided. This was just a continuation of tactics used by prison administrators throughout the world.

In the pressure of the prison environment, it was hard to avoid personal clashes. The enforced proximity caused a lot of friction. Only the residue of military discipline among the prisoners prevented it from becoming worse than it was.

Sources

1. *They Have Their Exits,* Airey Neave, London, Coronet Books, 1953, p. 55.

2. *The Third Sex,* Edited by Isadore Rubin, M.D., NY, New Book Company, 1961, pp. 82-85.

3. *Colditz, The Full Story,* P. R. Reid, NY, St. Martin's Press, 1984, pp. 108-110.

4. *They Have Their Exits,* pp. 68-69.

Part II

5

Escape and Evasion

The U. S. Armed Forces Code of Conduct states explicitly in Article III that "I will make every effort to escape and to aid others to escape." Other countries have similar rules.

In practice, escape is very difficult. Experience in several wars has shown that the prisoner's best chances are during the immediate period after his capture, before the captor has had the opportunity to get very organized. During this initial period, the potential escaper is close to his own lines, and the immediate battlefield area is typically confused, giving him the best chance to slip away unseen.

Evasion on the battlefield is a matter of luck, speed, basic fieldcraft, and cunning. The ability to make a quick decision and then "go for it" is crucial, because there's no time for long-term planning. In some cases, such as shot-down airmen, helicopter rescues can get them out before they're captured.[1]

At times, evasion can be spectacular. In 1944, a party of 138 Allied airmen hid in the woods near Chateaudun, in France, for months, evading the Germans. They had been sheltered and fed by the French underground. After the Normandy invasion, in 1944, a squadron of Special Air Service troopers penetrated the German lines and rescued them, bringing them back to Allied lines in a motorcade.[2]

Ground troops can avoid being captured, in certain situations, by several means. They can continue to resist. Sometimes, holding out a day or more enables friendly forces to come to the rescue. If the position is indefensible, breaking out to friendly territory is another choice. A breakout can be by the entire unit, or it can break up into small parties to allow infiltration. Another choice is to penetrate more deeply into enemy territory to act as a guerrilla unit. This tactic can work well when there's a fluid front or when fighting in friendly territory.[3]

Who Escapes?

Not every prisoner tries to escape. Most captives, criminal and military alike, are content to sit and serve their time. In civil life, a recaptured escapee gets an additional sentence tacked on to his time. Military escapees are not, in principle, punished for doing what is truly their duty, but in practice this isn't so. The Geneva Convention of 1929 permits a maximum punishment of thirty days in solitary confinement for trying to escape. However, the Japanese, although on the surface observing the Geneva Convention, used to execute recaptured escapees routinely. The Germans, after the embarrassing mass escape from Stalag Luft III, saw to it that recaptured escapees were "shot while trying to escape."

One authority claims that a rebellious nature is important.[4] This may or may not be true. Rebels are not usually found in the armed forces. Modern techniques of discipline suppress rebellious tendencies and weed out those that the "system" can't handle. The modern armed forces are schools for conformism. The explanation surely lies elsewhere.

The basic personal requirements are strong will and initiative, and the ability to plan and carry out a plan. Also important are morale in general, and faith in the rightness of one's cause. This is why escapees tended to be fanatics. Typically, die-hard Nazi's comprised the German escapees. The German press probably had similar terms for Allied escapees.

Another reason was boredom from enforced idleness. Life in a prison or POW camp is monotonous. In criminal prisons, monotony is part of the punishment. In POW camps, monotony simply happens because there are no facilities for the amusement of the prisoners.

Armed forces training often included some instruction on techniques of evasion and escape. One example is the U.S. Army Field Manual FM 21-77 and its classified supplement, FM 21-77A, and the courses based on them. It's hard to pin down what good any of these did, as there have been few American evadees in recent wars, and no escapees at all.

In World Wars I and II, there were comparatively many escapes from German and British POW camps. In absolute numbers they were few, but compared to what happened in Korea and Vietnam, they were significant.

Escapes varied from unplanned walk-aways and run-aways to elaborate schemes that took months to put into effect. In one case, a French doctor and priest were allowed to go for a walk in the woods with only one guard for a group of five. The doctor and priest ran for it, and made it as far as Saarbrucken, where the Germans recaptured them. Another run-away escape occurred when a party of five POWs were marched into town to go to the dentist, escorted by only two guards. By the time they were ready to return to camp, evening had come, with fog and a light rain. Suddenly, three POWs broke and ran down the street. The guards could not run after them, having others to guard, and they couldn't open fire in the middle of town without seeing their targets clearly.[5]

Another incident was a simple walk-away. Two French officers dressed as laborers walked out the camp gate. A genuine laborer was coming in, and not recognizing the two as fellow workers, asked the guard to detain them. The game was up.[6]

Those who wound up in camps would either settle in for the duration, or begin planning escapes. The planning, and the tools and techniques they used, are the next part of this study.

Sources

1. *Prisoners of War,* A. J. Barker, NY, Universe Books, 1975, p. 159.

2. *They Have Their Exits,* Airey Neave, London, Coronet Books, 1953, pp. 156-157.
3. *Evasion And Escape,* Field Manual 21-77, Washington, DC, Headquarters, Department of the Army, 1958, pp. 25-43.
4. *Prisoners of War,* A. J. Barker, NY, Universe Books, 1975, p. 147.
5. *Colditz, The Full Story,* P. R. Reid, NY, St. Martin's Press, 1984, p. 106.
6. *Ibid.,* p. 129.

6

Planning the Escape

Planning an escape requires deciding which technique to use. There are two basic types of escape; structural and "walk-aways." A walkaway is exactly that. A trustee or POW on parole or work-furlough walks away and does not return. Another type of walk-away is from a situation that does not demand parole, such as a work party. Walking away from a road gang or harvesting party requires waiting until the guard is distracted or otherwise inattentive.

A structural escape means breaching the physical security of the prison or camp. There are three basic methods of getting beyond the wire or walls: over, under, or through.[1]

Getting over the wall is one way. This can be by ladder or by climbing. Some have used helicopters.

Going under means a tunnel. This can be started from scratch and digging through the earth, or exploiting an existing drainpipe.

Going through means either slipping through by stealth or disguise, or forcing a way through, such as cutting the wire, and depending on speed to avoid getting shot.

Anyone planning an escape must first get a realistic idea of his chances of success. Although there have been many escape books written, all glorify the escapers and few note how slim the odds really were. Let's take a realistic look at what the odds might be:

In Colditz, the German "bad boys' camp," there were 84 escapers in 1942. Of these, only 16 made it.[2] The majority of Colditz prisoners didn't even try. The percentage who did try was much larger than in other German POW camps, because Colditz was reserved for those who had made attempts at other camps and for a few others whom the Germans considered especially dangerous. Also, Colditz was for officers. Experience showed that enlisted men rarely attempted escape.

The prison's physical structure is only the first obstacle. The surroundings are even more important. Breaking free is one thing. Staying free is another. That depends on blending in with the population outside the wire or walls and making the journey to a safe place.

Breaking out of a criminal prison is generally very difficult, but remaining free after the break is relatively easy because the escapee is in his own country and, unless he's "public enemy number one," won't have many police officers looking for him. One well-known American criminal escapee, for example, engineered his escape by a ruse. He had his captors take him out of prison to a site in a rural area, where he claimed to have hidden stolen jewelry. Actually, he had ditched a revolver with a broken firing pin. When the party, including three FBI Agents, arrived at the site, the escapee retrieved his inoperative revolver and bluffed his way out of their custody.[3]

A military POW camp is another problem. The physical escape is often easier, but the escaped prisoner is in a hostile country, and may not even speak the language. If, as in Korea and Vietnam, he's in a place populated by people of a different race, he can't possibly hope to walk freely among them. He can't show himself in public, use public transport, and often can't even move except at night.

This is why there were no successful escapes in Korea and Vietnam.[4] Physical security in the camps was not exceptionally tight, but there was practically no hope of traveling to friendly territory once outside the wire. Even the best forged documents could not transform "John Smith" into "Luc Nguyen Tho."[5]

Although Germans and Russians are both Caucasian, there were no successful escapes from Russian POW camps during World War II.[6]

No doubt, the vast distance between the camps and friendly territory played a role.

In occupied countries, the population would often help, or at least not denounce the escapee. Even in Asia during World War II, some prisoners were able to make their way out of occupied territory.[7]

Allied prisoners in Germany during WWI had a more encouraging prospect than during WWII. Holland was neutral in that war, and any escapee who managed to get over the Dutch frontier and who made his way to an Allied legation would have his repatriation assured. The Dutch would help him, if he could not find his way around their country. In WWII, however, Holland was an occupied country and the escaper was not home free if he crossed into Holland.

In the occupied countries, there were "escape lines" or "rat lines" organized, on the order of the "underground railways" which provided for escaped slaves in the United States before the Civil War. These escape lines were largely organized by MI-9, the British escape organization. They provided escapers with food and shelter. They also provided false papers and clothing suitable for the area. Other supplies and services they made available to escapers were medical care, native guides, local currency, and maps, if necessary.

Understandably, the Gestapo tried very hard to penetrate them, and one of their methods was to send a "ringer" down the line. This is why members of these organizations were very paranoid with their charges, and would screen them carefully. They also practiced tight security by keeping their escapee's knowledge of the lines as small as possible.[8]

Another problem faced the escaper. It sometimes happened that the Gestapo had arrested and "turned" a member of an escape line. This person would then work for the Gestapo, passing information and leading escapees into traps.

Switzerland had a common frontier with Germany, but during WWII, was completely surrounded by Axis controlled territory. WWI escapees could cross into Switzerland and then re-cross into France, but the situation during WWII was far more grim. The Germans had microphones buried along certain stretches of their frontier, and France was occupied territory. Also, the Swiss were forced to take their neutrality seriously, surrounded as they were by the Axis powers, and avoided any actions which seemed to show sympathy towards the Allies.

Another problem was that the frontier between Germany and Switzerland was extremely convoluted. One French officer, escaped from camp, tried to reach Switzerland and was recaptured. At one point while he was negotiating the frontier, a small boy walking in the woods spoke to him in French, but he did not reply. During his interrogation by a Gestapo officer, he found out that he had crossed into Switzerland, but inadvertently returned to Germany.[9]

Escape by sea was another possibility. During WWII, except for fliers shot down in France, there was no quick trip across the English Channel. Instead the Baltic dictated an escape by stowing away on board a neutral ship headed for Sweden. Norway, Denmark, and Finland were German-controlled.

Most often, escape had to be overland, blending in with the local population and using roads and rails to get across occupied territory and to neutral or friendly territory. This usually required civilian clothing, identity documents, ration coupons, travel permits, and railway tickets. At times, there was also a special document needed to permit travel near a frontier zone.

Railway tickets were not worth forging because escapers could buy them so easily at the ticket counter in the station. If they didn't have enough money, or felt that they didn't want to go into the station proper, they could "ride the rails" and go by freight trains. There was always a risk of being run off by the railway police, but there was no truly safe way to travel, in any event.

Ration coupons were the least of the problems. Strange as it may seem to those who have not lived through that era, not everything edible was rationed at all times during the war. There were often ration-free meals served in restaurants even in Germany. These were not very good, often stews containing little or no meat, but they satisfied hunger. The alternative was to carry food on the journey, which many civilians did, anyway. Canned food from Red Cross packages served this purpose well.

Eating Red Cross food within sight of German civilians was unwise. Real chocolate, for example, was extremely rare in wartime Germany, and anyone eating a bar of this in a train station or compartment would attract much unwanted attention. The wrapper, especially, would be a give-away. Smoking foreign cigarettes would almost always invite unwanted attention because these were either a tip-off that the smoker was a POW or in the black market.

The Escape Committee

In principle, the prison camp inmates are still organized, and still under military discipline. Indeed, in most armed forces, they're under orders to set up their own military chain of command, including an escape committee, as soon as possible once they arrive at their permanent camp.

American servicemen who become POWs are required to set up a chain of command inside the camp. The prisoner's representative negotiates with the camp commandant or administrators regarding the POWs' welfare and other matters affecting the POWs. He oversees the distribution of food and supplies to ensure that everyone gets a fair share. He also assigns work details and other duties inside the camp. He may have several assistants for this. One of the most important duties is keeping the POWs' health up by encouraging simple sanitation measures and primitive medical techniques, which probably will be all that's possible under the circumstances.[10]

The escape committee is the secret arm of the POWs' organization. It plans and carries out escape preparations, decides upon the timing and composition of escape attempts, and coordinates attempts by various groups. All POWs planning escapes or wishing to take part in an escape plan should work through the escape committee. This is to avoid working at cross-purposes. The escape committee should have veto power over any escape attempt, to avoid one attempt's interfering with another and to allocate resources available where they'll do the most good.

The prisoners' government may have a special escape office set up to facilitate escape and evasion by captured members. During WWII, MI-9 served this purpose for the British. One example of the resources this office marshaled was the set of plans for Colditz castle sent from Britain to help the POWs plan their escapes.[11]

The Germans also had an escape organization. At Camp Lethbridge, in Canada, German POWs had their own camp committees set up, with constant communication by radio and by mail with the "Fatherland."[12]

The U. S. Armed Forces also have such an organization, but not much about it has leaked out because it's classified. Paragraphs 6, 7, and 8 of U. S. Army Field Manual 21-77A deal with exactly this, and what aid the prison escape committee can expect.

During the Vietnam War, the U. S. Air Force had an organization known as the "1127th Field Activities Group." One of its divisions was the "Evasion and Escape Branch," which collected information on conditions in North Vietnam and advised airmen on evasion and escape.[13]

The most secret aspect of this type of organization is the "escape officer" sent into camps to maintain POW morale, assure their continued loyalty, and help organize escapes. There were such efforts in WWII, but these were so highly classified that no information on them has yet appeared in public media at this late date. The escape officer was essentially a political commissar, although he did not go by that title. This job required an unusually dedicated type of person, who would allow himself to be captured and who would then masquerade as an ordinary POW. He would bring news from home, and make contact with the escape organizations in the camps through which he passed.

In Europe, it was fairly easy to infiltrate such personnel. They would simply parachute out of an aircraft over occupied territory, posing as downed fliers. Because of the great amount of activity in that theatre of operations, infiltration went unnoticed. In Korea and Vietnam, it wasn't as easy, because of the much smaller number of captured airmen. Arranging capture on the ground was too risky to work.

The Communists in both Korea and Vietnam reportedly infiltrated commissars into POW camps in the south. In Korea, they built up a very strong POW organization which finally started a riot and took the American prison commandant, General Dodd, hostage.[14]

The purpose behind infiltrating commissars was not to organize escapes but to keep prisoners ideologically pure. Many of the communist soldiers were draftees who cared little about communist ideology, and just wanted to survive the war. To them prison camp was salvation, and many did not want to be repatriated, at least during the Korean War.

The Personnel Inventory

There are always some POWs with civilian skills that are useful in escape attempts. Locksmiths, for example, can find ways to get through the enemy's locked doors. Carpenters can help with various construction projects, such as false walls. Electronic technicians can search for enemy "bugs" and neutralize them. Miners can dig escape tunnels. A former printer can work on forging documents.

It's important to catalog military skills. Military engineers are valuable whenever there's any sort of construction involved. This may be digging a tunnel or building scaling ladders. Also included in this number are machinists and machine operators of various sorts. Navy machinists' mates can operate lathes and other tools, and even build or improvise some. Armorers, of whatever branch of the service, have skill in making and handling small machine parts.

This is why it's important for the escape committee to have a catalog of every camp inmate's skills. Of course, this must not be written and open to capture. If it's in coded notation, it may be secure enough. The other choice is memorization. This isn't necessarily as difficult as it might seem.

In a camp with a thousand POWs, and an escape committee of ten officers, it's not hard to divide the specialties among the officers. One can be responsible for anything to do with tunnels, and know everyone with such skills. Another can be in charge of electricity and electronics. Part of his task is to know everyone with such a background. Likewise with photography and photographic skills, valuable in document forging.

Keeping the list of skills secret from the enemy is another reason to avoid speaking too much, even about casual subjects. If a POW lets slip, for example, that he was a locksmith before the war, the guards might see him as a security risk, and neutralize him.

The Intelligence Committee

Information about the camp, its guards, security measures, and surrounding areas is vital to escape planning. The escape committee must set up a sub-committee to gather and sort out all sorts of information to help escape planning. Some of the areas to cover, and methods of obtaining information, are as follows:

- Prison layout. This is easy to obtain by simple observation. What's not as simple is information about sub-systems, such as electric wiring and plumbing, but POWs with experience in the construction trades often can help dope out this information. One use to which POWs can put this information is devising ways to knock out the camp's electricity, to shut down searchlights. Causing a power failure provides an opportunity for climbing the wire and getting away unseen.[15]

- New construction is always important. The construction site almost always offers an opportunity for disposing of dirt from tunnels under construction. If the construction involves towers, or anything at or close to the fence, there may be a weakening in physical security worth exploiting. Construction within the compound may bring workmen in through the gates, and with them opportunities for escape by impersonation. Construction sites also offer opportunities for stealing tools and materials. Digging implements are useful for tunnels. Electric wire serves for running electric lights down into a tunnel.

- Guard schedules. Again, simple observation can reveal shift changes, patrol areas, and other information. Points to watch here are timing of patrols and beats. A guard walking his beat may have a blind spot at one end or the other, and timing his speed reveals how long a particular spot or area remains unobserved. Keeping a 24-hour watch is essential, because the picture may change drastically at night. Timing of searchlight patterns is important to know. Also some guards don't patrol as watchfully at night. Others may reveal a tendency to doze. The guard commander may put on extra roving patrols at night, to counter the increased security risk. The weather is also important because a blinding fog, rain, or snowstorm may reduce visibility enough to make climbing the wire possible. A snowstorm will also fill in any tracks the escaper leaves behind him. Escape in a snowstorm happened at least twice in Germany.[16]

- Learning what the prison administration's emergency plan entails is important in planning escapes. It's important to know how the administration strengthens the defenses after an escape attempt, whether or not there are tracking dogs employed, the size of the party sent out after the escapees, and how far out the alert goes. Unfortunately, it's almost impossible to find out all of the ramifications without having an actual escape. A dummy run, as described below, can disclose some details.

- Getting to know individual guards is important. The intelligence committee should get a "feel" of which guards can be helpful. Help can come in the form of information about conditions outside. Guards can advise about train schedules, identity documents needed, and special travel permits. Keeping up casual conversations with guards can reveal many important facts that POWs need to plan an escape.

- Corrupting guards is a high-priority task. It's often possible to start the process by friendly conversations with guards. In cases where the POW parcels contain items scarce in the enemy economy, it may be possible to help the process by small gifts, such as coffee, cigarettes, and chocolate. In certain cases, the guards themselves may initiate the relationship by offering to buy these items. The exchange must be in the country's legal currency, not camp scrip, to enable building up a supply of escape money. The exchange can also take other forms, such as items that the camp administration considers contraband. Guards may trade inks and other printing supplies, cameras and film, or lend their personal documents to serve as models for forgeries.

- Close observation of visitors to the camp or prison can develop many tangible benefits. In any prison there are visitors on official duties, who are not part of the prison staff. These can include doctors and dentists, and various other contractors. If an electrician enters the perimeter to do repair work, his tool kit is worth stealing. This may not always be possible, especially if there's a guard with him, but sometimes it's possible to make off with one tool, such as a wire cutter, undetected, or to steal or borrow his pass. In some cases, it's possible to get out of a prison by disguising oneself as a workman.

- An important aspect of information-gathering is eavesdropping. Prison guards and administrators will often speak freely in the presence of POWs if they think the POWs can't understand their language. This is why the Intelligence Committee must promote the idea among all camp inmates never to reveal to any enemy they they speak or understand his language. At the same time, there should be crash courses among the POWs to teach the basics of the enemy tongue. This allows more POWs to be assigned to lounge around guard posts or wherever enemy guards are likely to gather and speak, to learn what they can.

- Current events and news from home are vital to maintain morale. This is why the Intelligence Committee should "debrief" every new arrival. Getting the latest war news can help, as can obtaining news from back home.

- Spotting "plants" is another reason for careful debriefing. Close questioning about conditions at home can help reveal the person posing as an American. It's also important to note that it's far more likely to encounter a genuine American who's turned informer than a fake American.

- Gathering news of conditions outside the wire is essential. Escapers need to know what passes and ID documents are necessary, and where the risks of discovery are least. It helps to know train schedules, and the likelihood of traffic police making vehicle checks on the roads. Road maps are important to anyone contemplating travel by car or bicycle. A simple, but vital, detail is whether or not it's necessary to show identity or vehicle papers when buying fuel.

Counter-Intelligence

Keeping security requires effective counter-intelligence, as well as the normal security measures such as "need-to-know." The counter-intelligence function will often be the intelligence officer's responsibility.

One step to help defeat the enemy's intelligence methods is to keep track of information, and observe how the guards react to events within the camp. If, as soon as anyone starts a tunnel entrance, the guards descend upon it, there's reason for considering a "leak." The leak may not be a traitor or informer. It may simply be sloppy security.

If it seems as if there's an informer within the camp, one technique for finding him is to concoct a story, such as that a new tunnel is starting, and to plant this story with different suspects. Each suspect gets a different version of the story. One may be told that the tunnel entrance is in the kitchen. Another that it's in the latrine. Observing where the guards search discloses which version of the story they've heard.

This game can become very subtle. A camp security officer may, to conceal his source, order his guards to search several different places before going to the actual one. This is why it's important to form an estimate of the security officer's competence and deviousness before coming to any conclusions.

Dealing With Informers

One extraordinarily unpleasant aspect of administering the camp is dealing with informers. One documented case comes from Colditz, in Germany. This concerned a Lieutenant Ryszard Bednarski, court-martialed by the Polish officers for betraying them to their captors. It turned out that Bednarski was not even a Polish officer, but had been infiltrated by the Germans to spy on them. He had apparently been threatened by the Germans, who suggested that they would harm his family if he didn't work for them as an informer.[17]

After the court-martial, the Senior British and Polish Officers went to the Commandant of Colditz to advise him that Bednarski's life would henceforth be in danger, as his fellow Poles planned to execute him by throwing him out of a high window.[18]

On the other side, there was the case of the German U-boat sailor Werner Drechsler, who had been a seaman aboard U-118 when the boat was sunk and the crew captured. After his rescue by the U.S. Navy, he apparently agreed to cooperate with Naval Intelligence officers in their efforts to glean information from members of U-boat crews. At the interrogation center at Fort Meade, Maryland, Drechsler played the role of informer, using the cover identity of "Petty Officer Leimi." He shared cells with various former U-boat crewmen, and in conversation managed to "pump" them for information that his controllers wanted. At some point he must have blown his "cover," because he was transferred to the POW camp at Papago Military Reservation, just East of Phoenix, Arizona, on March 12, 1944. Within a day he was dead. This camp held U-boat crews, including some from U-118, and apparently word of Drechsler's treachery had gone before him. His fellow POWs hanged him in the shower room.[19]

There are probably many more cases than these, but undiscovered because the trials and executions were carried out in secret. Reprisals against informers had to be kept secret from the camp administration for obvious reasons. There was also danger of revealing the events after the war, if any participants survived. Many of these courts-martial did not follow proper procedure, and would not have stood up to legal review by a higher court. This would have put the participants in difficult positions, possibly even leading to charges of murder. For these and other reasons, it was best to "let sleeping dogs lie."

It's also important to note that, according to the U. S. Army manual on escape and evasion, informers may also "report on rackets or other criminal activity conducted among the prisoners themselves and not necessarily directed against the captors." In a camp, not all POWs will be upright and honest, and some will try to better themselves by victimizing their fellow POWs. The camp administration will often try to suppress this, but it's more effective if the POW organization copes with the problem.

In certain cases, such as in Korea and Vietnam, the grip of the guards was so tight that the prisoner organization, such as it was, had no chance to do very much about anything. Individual prisoners simply noted names, and denounced the informers and traitors upon return to the United States. This led to several well-publicized trials after Korea, and some lesser-known court-martials after Vietnam.

Where the prisoner organization is strong, there can be an immediate effort to deal with informers and traitors. If the crime isn't very serious, there may be a warning, ostracism, corporal punishment, or threats of reprisals. In a couple of instances, the prisoners' senior officer appealed to the camp commandant to have the offender transferred for his own good. As we've already seen, there have been cases in which the informer did a great deal of damage, and was tried and executed inside the camp.

The prisoners' committee also dealt with other disciplinary problems. One noted affair of WWII was the case of the German submarine U-570, which its commander, Rahmlow, surrendered intact to the British in August, 1941. The prisoners at the camp in Britain where Rahmlow wound up would not speak with him, and an informer told the British administration that Rahmlow would soon face a "court of honor" for trial and possible execution. The British transferred him quickly into an air force camp.[20]

Reconnaissance

Once the escape committee decides upon a tentative plan, there must be a "feeling out" of the circumstances which falls under the heading of reconnaissance. If the plan is to cut the wire, it's important to know how the escapers will do this without being seen by guards. If the plan is to dig a tunnel under the wire, an important detail is where the tunnel will exit outside the wire. Often simple observation will provide the information needed. Sometimes, it's necessary to have a trial run to see if this trips whatever security system the guards have set up. A dummy run can also disclose security measures previously unknown to the prisoners.

Other details of the plan can be only tentative until the escape committee verifies them with a trial run. An important detail is getting rid of the diggings. Finding out if it's possible to deposit them in the yard inside the wire is workable without compromising a real tunnel. Digging a shallow hole under a barrack building will provide enough subsoil to test out the theory.

If the escape is to be at night, some part will probably call for crossing an open area theoretically under observation by guards. In the camps with curfews, guards are alert for prisoners in the open after curfew. They often use searchlights and foot patrols to cover the ground.

In many cases, searchlights don't cover all sides of the buildings thoroughly. There are bound to be many shadows, in which escapees can hide. Putting together an escape plan depends both on timing the searchlights and taking advantage of the cover provided by shadows.

A large open area is the hardest to cross because it has the least cover. Still, there is often "dead ground" caused by slight unevenness of the terrain. Tree stumps also throw hard shadows under the searchlights' glare.[21]

During the era before electronic night vision scopes, searchlights were the only devices available for piercing the dark, and they had severe limitations. Whatever the searchlight pattern and timing, guards will be handicapped by loss of night vision. They also develop a mental "blind spot" if they depend upon searchlights. They tend to see only what's outlined in the beam, even on a moonlit night. This provides many opportunities for rushing across open areas without being spotted.

Passive night vision scopes, which amplify existing light, are far more dangerous because they don't, unlike searchlights, indicate when an area is under observation. Thermal imaging devices are even more dangerous to escapers because they detect body heat, and can see a trail of heat left by an escaping prisoner. They can also "see through walls" in the sense that they detect the heat coming through a wall from the escaper's body on the other side.

Planning: The First Step

Obviously, planning is vital, especially when the guards make an effort to keep information from the prisoners. Having every detail worked out in advance helps greatly once the escape is underway. However, planning itself won't get the escaper very far without tangible preparation.

Sources

1. *Escape From Germany,* Aidan Crawley, NY, Simon and Schuster, 1956, p. 16.

2. *Colditz, The Full Story,* P. R. Reid, NY, St. Martin's Press, 1984, p. 181.

3. *Hacksaw,* Edward R. Jones, NY, Donald I. Fine, Inc., 1988, pp. 9-16.

4. *Prisoners of War,* A. J. Barker, NY, Universe Books, 1975, p. 149.

5. *The Raid,* Benjamin F. Schemmer, NY, Avon Books, 1976, p. 10.

6. *Prisoners of War,* A. J. Barker, p. 149.

7. *Ibid.,* p. 158.

8. *Evasion And Escape,* Field Manual 21-77, Washington, DC, Headquarters, Department of the Army, 1958, pp. 72-73.

9. *Colditz, The Full Story,* p. 67.

10. *Evasion And Escape,* pp. 96-104.

11. *Colditz, The Full Story,* p. 119.

12. *U-Boats, A Pictorial History,* Edwin P. Hoyt, NY, McGraw-Hill Book Company, 1987 p. 117.

13. *The Raid,* Benjamin F. Schemmer, pp. 26-27.

14. *Prisoners of War,* A. J. Barker, pp. 177-179.

15. *Escape From Germany,* p. 17.

16. *Ibid.,* p. 17

17. *Escape From Colditz, (The Colditz Story),* P. R. Reid, NY, Berkley Books, 1952, p. 124.

18. *Colditz, The Full Story,* pp. 149-150.

19. *Prisoners of War,* Ronald H. Bailey, Chicago, IL, Time-Life Books, 1981, p. 165.

20. *U-Boats,* p. 100.

21. *Escape From Germany,* p. 54.

7

Preparations for Escape

Preparations for the classic escape can be extensive and time-consuming. By definition, there's often less preparation needed for the impulsive or impromptu escape.

Tools and Supplies

Depending on how elaborate the escape will be, there may be many tools and supplies needed. In certain POW camps, prisoners went to great lengths to gather their personal escape kits. Colditz Castle, the German "bad boys' camp," was a gathering point for inveterate escapees who spent their otherwise idle hours preparing for the next escape. They copied maps of the area by tracing, manufactured home-made compasses, and accumulated some German currency. Others forged identity documents. Yet others made items of civilian clothing, such as caps, coats, and rucksacks.[1]

Prisoners in many cases manufacture, scrounge, or steal what they need. Many items are available for improvisation, such as eating utensils doubling as cutting or digging tools. Escapees from criminal prisons make do with what they can manufacture in the prison machine shop. The classic "saw in a birthday cake" smuggled in to the prisoner is now a joke. Almost nobody even tries that one anymore. However, during WWII, one POW tried to escape by sawing his bars with a saw smuggled in to him in a bottle of wine.[2]

Stealing tools is worth the effort. Prison machine shops have assortments of tools, some of which are vulnerable to theft. Although any well-run security system includes a count of all tools, it's still possible to improvise a dummy tool to take the place of the genuine article during the count. This is possible because the count is exactly that; a count by the numbers only, without close inspection of each article.

Another source of supplies is the guards. In some situations, POWs are better off than their captors. In criminal prisons, affluent criminals have assets far exceeding those of the staff, and associates outside the walls can pay off guards to smuggle contraband to the prisoners. One American traded his American cigarettes to a guard for a camera and film.[3]

In some POW camps, such as Colditz, prisoners had food items that were either rationed or unavailable in Germany, and were able to trade with the guards. In many cases, they simply sold bars of chocolate and accepted German money instead of camp scrip. One German guard supplied tools to the prisoners over a period of time, apparently running a small business this way. German authorities discovered this, and court-martialed and shot him.[4]

POWs have more resources behind them. Their government may supply them with certain items. The British organization, MI-9, devised a basic escape kit for British servicemen. This consisted of a compass, maps, and concentrated food at the start. Later developments brought some very sophisticated refinements.

Cans of food found in parcels from home are very helpful, because they serve as escape rations. This is why POW camp officials puncture cans of food before giving them to the prisoners. There are other items sent which are explicitly escape aids, and which camp officials would confiscate or destroy if they discovered them:

- Clothing with buttons containing tiny compasses.
- Canned food with false bottoms containing escape gear.

- Canned food with double walls containing paper contraband, such as money.
- False documents, including ID cards, ration coupons, and travel permits.
- Materials for forging documents.
- Enemy money.
- Maps of the area.
- Radios.
- Saws.

Parcels from home were regular sources of escape materials. The government escape organizations set up several "fronts" for distributing escape materials hidden in ordinary items sent to POWs. Some of the items smuggled in were:

- Compasses and hacksaw blades in hollow tennis rackets.
- Phonograph records with maps and money under the labels.
- Playing cards with maps laminated in them.
- Chess sets with hollow pieces.
- Toothbrushes containing hacksaws and screwdrivers inside their hollow handles.[5]

Such contraband has come not only in packages sent by the POW's family, but even in Red Cross parcels.[6]

Additional materials which prisoners used to aid their escapes were:

- Railroad maps and timetables.
- Railroad tickets.
- Articles of enemy uniforms.
- Civilian clothing.
- Dyes to convert their uniforms to the enemy color.
- Digging tools.
- Wire cutters.

Late in WWII, escape supplies were much more compact and pre-planned. The British escape organization, MI-9, arranged to send in concentrated food tablets, water-purifying tablets, and stimulant pills to keep the escaper going.[7]

Maps were printed on silk handkerchiefs. Razor blades sent to POWs were magnetized, to allow their use in improvised compasses.

The U.S. Armed Forces devised a series of "escape and evasion" kits which they issued to all service personnel in danger of capture. Most of these kits went to airmen, because they were the most likely to end up far behind enemy lines and cut off from help. A typical WWII-era kit contained:

- One compass.
- One signal mirror.
- One tube of halazone (water purifying) tablets.
- Three small bandages.
- Two sewing needles.
- Two safety pins.
- One small spool white thread.
- One single-edged razor blade.
- 6 waterproof matches.
- 10 yards nylon fishing line.
- 6 fish hooks.
- 6 flies.
- One instruction booklet.

This was as much of a "survival" kit as it was an escape kit. All of the items listed were packed in a plastic box measuring 3″ x 3″ x 1″ and sealed with waterproof tape. The kit was designed to fit into a small pocket on a jumpsuit.

Other kits issued during WWII contained items such as:

- Photographs (mug shots) to use on forged documents.
- German currency.
- Benzedrine tablets.
- Malted milk tablets.

- Chewing gum.
- Water bag.
- Adhesive tape.

More elaborate kits came after the end of the war. These contained larger quantities, and also included maps, drugs, food tablets, antibiotics, field dressings, and some contained rather exotic items. The kit issued to CIA pilot Francis Gary Powers contained a poison needle with which he could commit suicide if he didn't want to face capture. He also had a Hi-Standard .22 suppressor-equipped auto pistol.

Communications

POWs were sometimes able to communicate with their governments at home. In most cases, this was by codes concealed in ordinary-appearing letters.[8]

A plan to cover special situations came about near the end of the war in Europe. A group of parachutists known as the Special Allied Airborne Reconnaissance Force was to drop near POW camps not yet liberated, and set up contact with the POWs to arrange joint efforts for their liberation. Carrying a portable radio, they were prepared to arrange arms drops to equip the prisoners when the moment came to move.[9]

One of the most ambitious escape attempts involved an escape from Camp Lethbridge, Ontario, by members of Germany's U-Boat service. This required exact coordination between the prisoners, the escape organization inside Germany, and U-Boat headquarters. The plan was to have the escapees picked up by a U-Boat in the Saint Lawrence River. Unfortunately for the POWs, the plan proved too cumbersome to be workable.[10]

Preparations for escape involved not only gathering supplies, and coordinating the efforts among several POWs. They also required some tangible techniques, such as forging enemy documents and simulating his uniforms. We'll look at specific escape techniques next.

Sources

1. *Colditz, The Full Story,* P. R. Reid, NY, St. Martin's Press, 1984, p. 69.

2. *The Master Book of Escapes,* Donald McCormick, NY, Franklin Watts, Inc. 1975, p. 147.

3. *Prisoners of War,* Ronald H. Bailey, Chicago, IL, Time-Life Books, 1981, pp. 56-57.

4. *Colditz, The Full Story,* pp. 155-156.

5. *Prisoners of War,* Ronald H. Bailey, Chicago, IL, Time-Life Books, 1981, pp. 72-73.

6. *Prisoners of War,* A. J. Barker, NY, Universe Books, 1975, p. 233.

7. *They Have Their Exits,* Airey Neave, London, Coronet Books, 1953, p. 39.

8. *Colditz, The Full Story,* pp. 167-169, 333-334.

9. *Ibid.,* pp. 270-271.

10. *U-Boats, A Pictorial History,* Edwin P. Hoyt, NY, McGraw-Hill Book Company, 1987, p. 117.

8

Escape Techniques, A to Z

This is a quick survey of various tools and techniques useful to escapers. Some topics, such as tunnels, are so complicated that they require chapters to themselves.

Bars

Cutting through prison bars takes a saw harder than the steel used in the bars. Hacksaw blades usually work.

The escape often can't be timed to go with the last cuts in the bars. Disguising the cuts is often necessary to prevent discovery. This can be done by filling in the gaps with a mixture of bread, dirt, and water to blend in with the steel, or at least to cover the glint of white metal. It's also wise to leave some metal, so that if a passing guard grips the bar and shakes it, it won't come away in his hand. At the last moment, it's possible to kick the bar out.

Black Market

This covers goods illegally procured from corrupt guards, and material bought from the civilian population. The reason the black market can thrive is that some POWs have goods that members of the enemy population want. Chocolate and cigarettes come in Red Cross parcels, and are severely rationed in wartime. In one German POW camp, it was possible to buy an egg from local farmers for two cigarettes. The price for a two-pound loaf of bread was ten cigarettes. The market operated through the help and connivance of the guards. In many cases, guards would provide various types of contraband to the POWs.[1]

Civilian Clothing

This was important for escapees who wanted to blend in with the civil population. POWs came to camp with only their uniforms, but often had fresh clothing sent from home. Camp tailors, or the prisoners themselves, managed to convert some of this. One French escaper, Lieutenant Lebrun, converted a set of pajamas into a gray suit.[2]

The RAF uniform was easier than most to re-cut and re-shape to resemble a civilian suit. Changing the color with improvised dyes made from coffee or indelible pencil leads often helped to disguise its origin.

At times, sympathetic guards would bring in civilian clothing for the POWs. One brought them in by wearing them under his own clothes.[3]

Sometimes, it was possible to steal clothing. At Colditz, several POWs conspired to steal a Homberg hat and overcoat from a German dentist attending to the needs of some of the POWs.

One officer had been sent to a hospital, and stole a nurse's hat and cape from a hook on the wall. This officer went out into the street, with boots and a large black mustache, and was arrested shortly thereafter. This was not his finest hour.[4] Civilian clothing did not have to be perfect, or even fashionable. At the time, there were millions of foreign workers serving in "Total Einsatz" in Germany, and some of them wore very shabby clothing.

Codes

Sending coded messages home was a main objective of POWs. At the beginning of every war, some servicemen are instructed in codes and ciphers to use in case of capture. Most coding techniques involved ways of including the message in letters home. A very simple way to do this is to compose a letter with every fourth or fifth word as part of the "real" message. This is too simple to fool many censors, which made it necessary to find more elaborate systems.

Another, more complex method is to write out the message to be encoded and to assign numbers to each word in a prearranged pattern. This produces a list of words out of logical sequence. The writer then places them in his letter in a sequence determined by the date. For example, if the date is the 24th of the month, every 2nd, then 4th word is part of the message.

Covering Up Absences

When there was an escape, keeping the knowledge from the captors as long as possible would give the escapees a better head start before the alert went out to neighboring police and military posts. Prisoners developed a wide variety of methods to cover up absences.

Dutch officers in Colditz devised a method of fooling the Germans conducting the "appel," or line-up, after an escape. They lined up in ranks of five, and the Germans counted them twice, once from the front and once from the rear. Two rows, however, had only four men in them, and the Germans overlooked this.

Polish officers devised another tactic. They were quartered in several large dormitories, and covered up the absence of two of their number by making use of a secret hatchway between two of the rooms. At the appel, they claimed that four men were sick in bed. A German who went up to check found two Poles in bed in one room. As he went down the hall to the door of the second dormitory, the two Polish officers scrambled through the hatch and into beds in the second room. The German reported that he'd counted four sick in bed.[5]

Another technique was using dummies. This works both in military and criminal prisons. It was only necessary to make a bust of a person, and to drape a coat over the bust. On appel, keeping a dummy's head afloat at eye level, and placing a pair of uniform boots together under the dummy, will sometimes fool the guards, who aren't looking closely at each face but merely counting heads.[6]

In a cellblock, fooling the guard making the night count requires making a plaster head, pasting some hair on it, and stuffing pillows under the blankets. A guard passing at night might well take the dummy for a real person under the blankets.

If it's not possible to cover the absence of the escapees, there's another technique available. This is to hide several additional prisoners within the walls when a real escape occurs. Prison or camp administrators will think that more escaped than actually did, and when the prisoners in hiding don't show up they'll think that they made a clean get-away. When the excitement dies down, those in hiding make their escape, with nobody missing them and no intensified alert outside the wire.[7]

Yet another technique is the fake escape, with nobody actually getting through the wire but merely hiding inside the camp. This results in a general alert when the count comes up short. After a few days of search outside the camp, the assumption will be that the escapees made it, and prison administrators will call off the search. It is then that the escapees actually penetrate the wire and make their escape, without the handicap of a general alert. See "Ghosts."

Dogs

Tracking dogs, with extremely acute smell, are often used for recovering escapees. There are several ways of throwing them off the scent. One is by walking into a stream or river, and following it for a long distance up or down stream, to break the trail. Another is by urinating, which allegedly will induce the dog to urinate too, and spoil his tracking ability.[8]

Another technique is to saturate a handkerchief with ammonia, and drop it on the trail. The handkerchief will attract the dog or his handler, and once the dog smells the ammonia, his sense of smell is ruined for the day. A special mixture to serve the same purpose, but less obviously, was issued during WWII. This was powdered blood and cocaine. The dog would be attracted by the scent of blood, and when he came up to it would inhale the cocaine, which would anesthetize his olfactory sense for several hours.

Ghosts

These are prisoners who go into hiding to simulate an escape and who emerge only after the uproar has died down. They may hide independently, or at the same time as another escape, to fool the guards into thinking that more escaped than actually did.

Hacksaws

Using a hacksaw blade properly is vital, to reduce noise and to prolong the life of the blade. Lubrication reduces wear on the cutting edge. As the special cutting oil necessary isn't often available in prison, soap has to substitute.[9]

Figure 2

A traditional prison escape tool, the hacksaw blade must be lubricated to reduce noise and preserve the sharp cutting edge.

Handcuffs and Leg Irons

There are several ways to get out of these. The simplest is to have hands smaller than the wrists. Some people have this congenital characteristic, and they disguise it by spreading or bunching their hands when they're handcuffed. Left alone, they squeeze their hands together and the cuffs slip off.

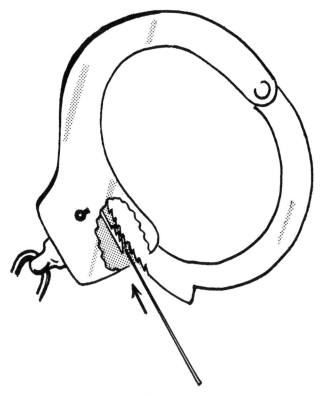

Figure 3

One way to pick handcuffs is to wedge a piece of spring steel between the teeth and ratchet.

Picking the locks is also possible, and much easier than many realize. One way is to slip a piece of thin flat spring steel between the shackle teeth and the locking ratchet, as shown in Figure 3 on page 72.

Another way is a hypodermic needle. Yet another is to use a ball-point pen refill, with one section cut and bent at right angles to substitute for the handcuff key (Figure 4).[10]

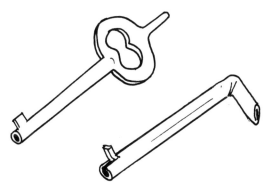

Figure 4

A brass ballpoint pen refill makes a handy lock pick for handcuffs.

Hides

Hides can serve for people or for inanimate objects. There were several escapes or attempts using hiding places beyond the walls. At Colditz, two Dutch officers assigned to an exercise detail used a sheet with leaves sewn to it to cover themselves as they lay in a shallow depression in the ground.[11]

Another hide that served well was a manhole cover over a well. The well was in the middle of a football field, and the officers formed a circle around it to screen it from view of their guards. Inside the circle, two officers pried open the cover and slipped inside. After the party had been marched back to the prison, they lifted the cover and escaped.[12]

POWs at Dulag Luft were often escorted to a playing field just outside the wire for exercise. There was a goat with a kennel on this playing field, and the goat soon became the officers' pet. They fed it and played with it. The officers decided to dig a hide for one man under the floor of the kennel, and cover up the absence during the count. They dug the hole gradually, carrying the dirt away on their persons. When the hide was ready, one officer hid inside and took off after the others had gone back inside the wire. He got as far as the Swiss border, where police arrested him.[13]

POWs building up a stockpile of escape gear needed places to store them securely, with minimal risk of discovery. One obvious storage place was inside a tunnel. In other cases, there were many hollows inside barracks walls, which prisoners exploited. If the barracks had dirt floors, digging small pits served the purpose. Other hiding places were holes dug within the camp compound.

There were hides built into everyday objects (Figure 5 on page 75). A game board was hollow, with escape money and maps in the secret compartment. Playing cards sent from England were laminated and came apart to reveal numbered map sections. When assembled, the sections gave a composite map of the occupied territories. A miniature compass was in a walnut shell. Spools of thread were hollow, containing tightly-rolled maps and other small contraband. A coat hanger had hollowed-out compartments. There were escape items such as maps, candy in cellophane, and a small compass cast into bars of soap. A checkerboard purportedly sent from Harrods, a British department store, contained forged German I.D.[14]

Finally, there were hiding places on the person, which were mostly useful when the guards did not do thorough body searches. A favorite place for medium-security hiding is in the rectum. Prisoners at Colditz used aluminum cigar tubes for this.[15]

Inmates of criminal prisons also have their hides. In the older prisons, there are loose bricks in the thick walls, and inmates store small items behind them. Prisoners working in any of the prison industries can find innumerable places to conceal contraband near their work stations. Those working on the prison farm can dig holes and bury their "stash." A deck of playing cards, with the cards' centers cut out, made a hiding place for drugs. A bible, with a section of the pages cut away, served to conceal a "shank."[16]

Figure 5

*Everyday items that don't attract attention
are often used as hiding places.*

Impersonation of Enemy Personnel

Tailoring uniforms to resemble German ones was a technique escapees repeatedly tried. Airey Neave, author of one classic escape book, related how he adapted a Polish tunic reshaped to resemble a German one, a dyed pair of RAF trousers, and various cardboard insignia painted with silver paint to try to pass as a German corporal. Unfortunately, when he tried to pass the gate one night, the scenery paint he'd used to color his tunic glowed green in the ultra-violet of the arc lights.[17]

The techniques of manufacturing German uniforms improved with time. One of the refinements was to use lead from pipes to cast buttons and insignia. It was possible to improvise molds for buttons, badges, and buckles from bars of soap.[18]

Uniform holsters had been made with cardboard at first, but later POWs used linoleum to simulate leather. Another good material was tar paper, scrounged from inside the wooden walls of barracks.

A more difficult task was creating dummy weapons. Anyone impersonating a German sentry had to have a rifle, and prisoner craftsmen simulated these with wood. They faked the metal parts by using lead pencil, rubbed into the wood grain and polished to give a metallic sheen. Some rifles were so realistic that it was possible to fix and remove the bayonet, and even open and close the bolt.[19]

In some cases, POWs impersonated German workmen. The most effective way to do this was to select a workman who closely resembled one of the prisoners. It was then necessary to procure similar clothing, a tool-bag, and the right pass. This could easily take months. In one case, a POW impersonated a chimney-sweep. He obtained a fake set of brushes and weights, and the required clothing, which included a top hat. When the chimney-sweep next came to the camp, the POW put on the clothing and walked out the gate, fooling the guard.

Incompetence of Guards

It often happens that guards don't do their jobs properly, leaving a gap in prison security. This is why alert prisoners can often find simple and obvious ways of escaping. In one case, a prisoner was able to bring two hacksaw blades, taped to the back of his forearm, into a federal prison because the intake guards did not search him adequately.[20] In other cases, guards or escorting officers became complacent and careless, and a prisoner was able to disarm them and escape.

Often, guards' mind-sets were such that it was possible to exploit intangible blind spots. One of the main objectives in a POW camp was to find a passage between the POW quarters and the camp staff's quarters or offices. This was because exits from the POW section were closely guarded, but exits from the guards' sections were not. Any sentry observing officers or enlisted men, wearing the proper uniforms, leaving from a staff exit wouldn't be likely to challenge them. The prisoners' theater at Colditz prison had a stage which passed over the German quarters, and prisoners broke through into the section and escaped by posing as German officers.

Prisoners setting out to impersonate Germans usually picked a time right after a shift change to make their attempts. This way, they reasoned, the guards would think that they had entered the camp during the previous shift, and not pay undue attention. In one case, three POWs impersonated a mission from the protecting power and their German officer escort. The three approached the gate, with two British senior officers speaking with them. They continued their discussion in front of the guard, then said their good-bys and turned to the gate. The guard did not even ask for their passes but opened the gate immediately.[21]

Invisible Inks

These provide one method of secret communication between prisoners and the outside. There are many ways of equipping a serviceman with invisible ink for use if captured. One is a handkerchief saturated with the chemical. Another is a tablet concealed in the hem of his jacket, or inside a coat button. Yet another is disguised as medicine. In certain cases, legitimate medicine can serve as invisible ink.

There used to be a headache remedy called "pyramidon," popular in Europe. Dissolving such a tablet in water produced invisible ink. The writer would use a toothpick or a cotton swab to write his message. It was important not to use a nib pen of the era, because this would disturb the surface of the paper with scratches. Development was with iodine fumes.

Another chemical, used in laxatives, is phenolphthalein. This is colorless as a powder or in water, but turns pink when exposed to an alkali. Sodium carbonate or sodium hydroxide will bring the writing out.

Ferrous sulfate also provides colorless writing. A solution of potassium cyanate brings it out. Copper sulfate crystals produce a medium blue solution which appears colorless on paper. Ammonia fumes develop the writing. Other secret inks are milk, lemon juice, vinegar, and urine, all of which develop with application of heat.

Locks and Keys

There have been many lock-picking tools devised, but one of the simpler methods is making a duplicate key from improvised materials. There have been many instances of POWs "borrowing" guards' keys and returning them after making impressions. In one case, POWs even stole keys from Gestapo agents.[22]

Mines and Minefields

There are some prison camps with minefields around them as extra layers of security. Minefields are cost-effective methods of enhancing security, but not very effective overall. The reason is that prisoners often can find out about them and avoid the traps. POWs often can watch the minefields being laid, and indeed some armies use POW labor to do this.

Such mines are always anti-personnel types. Some of these are "Bouncing Bettys," the sort that shoot a "submunition" up to chest or groin level before detonation. These almost always operate with a trip-wire that can be seen, but because many escapes are during darkness, it's very easy to trip one.

The POW escape committee can determine if there are minefields by watching how guards walk around outside the wire. It's also possible to find out about security measures from corrupt guards.

Streams around the camp may also be mined with "fluvial" mines or adaptations of ground mines. This is because walking or swimming in streams is a well-known method of eluding tracking dogs. If the area is populated, mines in streams are less likely because of the danger to civilians. One technique of using streams safely is to float a log down the stream before following at a safe distance. The log will trip fluvial mines.[23]

Money

In most prisons and POW camps, inmates are forbidden to have money because this could facilitate an escape once the escapee reached the outside world. Camp currency is some sort of scrip, totally unlike money, and not negotiable on the outside. German camp currency was called "Lagergeld." There were many efforts at obtaining enemy money.

One way was smuggling it in. One French officer, Lebrun, made a spectacular escape from Colditz Castle in 1941, and tried to use a German banknote that had come to him in a food parcel sent by a relative. Unfortunately, this banknote was obsolete, dating from the early 1920s, and when he tried to buy a railway ticket with it, it led to his arrest and recapture.

Enemy currency was included in many escape and evasion kits issued to airmen. The amounts varied, and sometimes included currency of several countries.

Another way of obtaining money was from the guards. During WWII, some POWs got money from their guards by selling them chocolate and other items from their Red Cross parcels.

Railroad Tickets

Buying railroad tickets was always a critical moment. All escapees who decided to travel by rail knew that this was when ignorance of local conditions or schedules might trip them up, or they might not have the proper papers if asked. Usually needed were identity cards and travel permits. They also had to ask for tickets to make the right connections if changing trains was necessary. They also found out through hard experience that asking for a ticket to a frontier zone meant that it was necessary to show a special pass for the frontier zone. Within the zone, it was necessary to show ID to get on or off a train.[24]

It was often better to buy a ticket for a town close to the frontier, but not quite in the special frontier zone. It might then be possible to take a commuter train, trolley, or even walk. Commuter trains were plentiful, at least in the early years of the war, and it wasn't usually necessary to show papers to buy tickets. It was only necessary to blend in with the many foreign workers.

It was a common misconception that the Gestapo patrolled trains and railway stations. The Gestapo, an elite counter-espionage police, had too few agents for this duty. Instead, railway police checked papers at train stations and on the trains themselves.

Layovers between trains could be dangerous because railway police checked papers at the stations. Anyone in a railway station waiting room who did not have a ticket would encounter close examination. Layovers also brought an opportunity to eat without ration coupons. The station restaurant often had a coupon-free meal in the early years of the war.

If it became necessary to leave the train station, a motion picture theater was a good place to stay for a few hours. It provided shelter from the elements in winter, darkness and relative freedom from observation and questioning, and even a place to doze if the escaper were very tired.

It was important not to fall asleep, especially for those who talked in their sleep. One escaping officer was lucky to have a partner who kicked him awake as he lay speaking in English as he dozed.[25]

Trap Doors

These served to conceal tunnel entrances and exits, and passages within and below buildings. One trap door was beneath the raised stage of the camp theater at Colditz. This was to hide access to a passageway leading to the attic over the German officers' quarters. This trap had to be made of wood, and with enough dust on it to appear untouched for years.

Trap doors made to conceal tunnel exits were shallow boxes resting on frames within the tunnel shaft. These boxes were filled with dirt to blend in with the surroundings. It was far more difficult to make a trap to conceal a tunnel exit in a grassy field.

Sources

1. *Escape From Germany,* Aidan Crawley, NY, Simon and Schuster, 1956, p. 238.

2. *Colditz, The Full Story,* P. R. Reid, NY, St. Martin's Press, 1984, p. 62.

3. *Escape From Germany,* p. 44.

4. *Ibid.,* p. 32.

5. *Colditz, The Full Story,* pp. 76-77.

6. *Ibid.,* pp. 92-93.

7. *Ibid.,* p. 77.

8. *The Master Book of Escapes,* Donald McCormick, NY, Franklin Watts, Inc., 1975, p. 148.

9. *Hacksaw,* Edward R. Jones, NY, Donald I. Fine, Inc., 1988, p. 257.

10. *Ibid.,* p. 171.

11. *Colditz, The Full Story,* pp. 104-105.

12. *Ibid.,* pp. 75-76.

13. *Escape From Germany,* pp. 30-31.

14. *Colditz: The Great Escapes,* Ron Baybutt, Boston, Little, Brown, And Company, 1982, pp. 64-67.

15. *Colditz, The Full Story,* p. 142.

16. *Improvised Weapons in American Prisons,* Jack Luger, Port Townsend, WA, Loompanics Unlimited, 1985, pp. 67-72.

17. *They Have Their Exits,* Airey Neave, London, Coronet Books, 1953, pp. 70-77.

18. *Prisoners of War,* Ronald H. Bailey, Chicago, IL, Time-Life Books, 1981, p. 98.

19. *Escape From Germany,* pp. 57-58.

20. *Hacksaw,* p. 255.

21. *Escape From Germany,* pp. 64-65.

22. *Escape from Colditz, (The Colditz Story),* P. R. Reid, NY, Berkley Books, 1952, p. 122.

23. *Evasion And Escape,* Field Manual 21-77, Washington, DC, Headquarters, Department of the Army, 1958, p. 78.

24. *Colditz, The Full Story,* p. 81.

25. *They Have Their Exits,* p. 94.

9

Forgery of Passes and I.D.

Forgery of ID was common among POWs during WWI and WWII. The main reason was that documents of the day were primitive, and very easy to forge or alter with low-tech materials. I.D. of the era was simple, and did not involve laminated cards or magnetic stripes. Forgery was far simpler, and it was possible to put together a set of false papers by hand. Some POWs had access to typewriters. In one camp, they built their own.

I.D. was necessary to exist in the occupied countries, and police made spot-checks on the streets to catch fugitives. These were routine, and entirely apart from the special alerts called when someone escaped from a POW camp. There were identity checks to catch Jews, underground workers, and Allied agents. I.D. checks would also help round up draft dodgers, as Germany had military conscription. For this reason, any fit man of military age was likely to attract attention.

It was also necessary to have one or more permits for travel. Public transportation was especially heavily policed. German trains had railway police scrutinizing I.D. on most trips. Civil aircraft were so tightly controlled that nobody even tried an escape on an airliner.

Many POWs could not speak the language of the country well enough to pass as natives. Fortunately, in wartime there are often many foreign workers, and impersonating one of these was safer than trying to pass as a native. The documents were also somewhat different. A foreigner identity card and work permit were essential, but any irregularity in these was easier to explain away because foreigners could always pretend to be stupid, which catered to the natives' prejudices, anyway. This made impersonating a foreign worker easier.

It was sometimes possible to generate fake I.D. from scratch. This required a model, which was a pass stolen or borrowed from a visitor or guard. If a visitor, such as a workman, hung his coat up while he was working, a POW would soon sidle up and frisk the pockets, looking for something to steal or borrow. If the pocket contained a pass of the sort needed to get out of the prison, forgers would make a hurried copy before the workman left.[1]

Another choice was to alter stolen or bought documents. One way of erasing the ink, used before ball point pens became popular, was potassium permanganate. This is an oxygen bleach that, in a dilute solution, will bleach some inks. This was sometimes obtainable from the camp hospital, where it was an ingredient in a gargling solution.[2]

Although pens, inks, and especially stamp-pad ink and stencil blocks were forbidden to the prisoners, some German guards were approachable and would smuggle these in to prisoners in return for chocolate, cigarettes, or other scarce supplies. One even brought in photographic materials for the prisoners' use. Prisoners would also manufacture their own forgery tools, using linoleum or shoe soles as stencil blocks.

There was a section of the POW organization devoted to obtaining or making fake I.D. Later in the war, some POWs arrived with several small passport photographs of themselves in civilian clothing, taken and issued to them in anticipation of use in forged documents. These formed part of their escape kit, which was not always confiscated by their captors.

The government escape organization took extensive steps to provide prisoners with means of forging I.D. In one case, a "complete chemical photographic laboratory" was discovered by the Germans in a parcel sent from England.[3]

In another case, an unwitting German officer gave the POWs help in preparing their I.D. photos. He allowed them to borrow his Contax camera to take photographs of a play the prisoners were staging. The POWs had the camera for half a day, according to German court-martial records, and thus had the opportunity to remove the film, insert film of their own smuggled from Britain, and take their I.D. mug shots. Afterwards, they were able to replace the original film in the camera.[4]

In some cases, prisoners had outside help in obtaining photographs. At Oflag XXIB, at Schubin, a Polish girl living nearby was a friend of a Polish RAF officer. She sent a camera into camp via a Polish worker. The prisoners took their own photographs, which the girl had developed and printed, and sent back in.

In some cases, it was possible to invent passes. The German administration had issued so many passes and identity documents that it was difficult to know all of them, and new ones were coming out regularly. This made it workable to concoct an authoritatively worded document that would pass inspection in most cases. However, the major point in manufacturing a pass from scratch was fluency in official German. Official documents have a certain syntax, very unlike conversational language, and any forged documents must be worded in the correct "officialese."

Raw materials for making fake documents were available from several sources. Toilet paper worked for tracing. Good quality typing paper was available in the camp office, from which a POW might steal it. POWs also received artists' materials and supplies from home, including assortments of drawing papers, inks and paints, and brushes. Water-colors were especially valuable for tinting forgeries that had to be specific colors. Thick drawing paper made good identity cards.[5]

Forging printed documents was difficult, taking careful hand work. The tools gradually became more available, with mapping nibs and pen-holders sent from home. Artists' brushes allowed many types of detail work, but required both skill and patience.

In one case, a German guard helped the POWs with typing. He took the drafts with him on leave and typed stencils on his wife's machine.[6]

The technique of forging a rubber stamp was to draw an outline of the stamp required on a piece of rubber heel or linoleum with white ink, as shown in Figure 6. It was then possible to cut out the design using a razor knife, which was often improvised from pieces of razor blades set in crude handles.

Figure 6

*The heel of a shoe becomes a forger's tool,
as official seals are "engraved" into the rubber.*

Fortunately for the forgers, German stamps tended to be very similar, with the common pattern for a police stamp being a circle with the German eagle in the center. The name of the jurisdiction was printed around the periphery.

It was also necessary to forge the stamp of the local labor office, which issued travel permits to workers. These were somewhat different, but still possible to forge.

Small details combined to trip up escapees who did not do their homework. A travel permit had to have, for example, the signature of the town commandant or local police official. Getting the name right was a major problem, and some who forged the wrong signature did not pass the first police check. At times, frontier zones required special permits of their own, and anyone without one was subject to arrest.

This was what complicated the forgers' tasks. In one case, for example, officers escaping from Schubin, in Poland, needed an assortment of passes to get to their destinations. During the first stage, they used papers proclaiming them to be Polish workers. Near the coast, they discarded the Polish papers and used I.D. stating that they were Danish seamen. Their cover story was that their ship had sunk, and that they'd lost all of their papers at sea. They carried only temporary passes for foreign workers from the Danish consulate in Danzig. These were letters authorizing them to travel to Denmark to obtain new papers. They also carried letters from an imaginary German office in Danzig authorizing their travel.[7]

The forging techniques of those days were adequate for the era. Today, it would be almost impossible to produce passable forgeries of most I.D. documents. They'd have to be stolen.

Sources

1. *Escape From Germany,* Aidan Crawley, NY, Simon and Schuster, 1956, p. 59.

2. *The Master Book of Escapes,* Donald McCormick, NY, Franklin Watts, Inc., 1975, p. 51.

3. *Escape From Germany,* p. 290.

4. *Ibid.,* p. 289.

5. *Ibid.,* pp. 60-61.

6. *Ibid.,* p. 61.

7. *Ibid.,* pp. 62-63.

10

Tunnels

This is possibly the most absorbing and over-dramatized escape technique in history. While many tunnels were ingenious in overall concept or in details, the success rate was low. Royal Air Force POWs in Germany had a one in 35 chance of success by digging tunnels.[1] Even then, few who got out via tunnel made it home. Another problem was that tunnels have always been labor-intensive. Digging a tunnel is not something that one or two escapers can carry out unaided. During WWII, when tunnelling was at its peak, it took a crew to dig a tunnel successfully. As we'll see when we examine each aspect closely, each tunnel project needed diggers, look-outs, and other personnel, who had to remain on duty for many hours each day.

Another problem was security. A basic principle of maintaining security is that the more people in on a secret, the less secure the secret can be. This is why it's vital to restrict knowledge of a secret project to those with a "need to know." A tunnel involves so many people, all of whom have a need to know, that it's virtually impossible to maintain total security. Despite this, POWs have been digging tunnels for many years.

Tunneling has a long history, dating at least back into the last century. During our Civil War, 109 Union officers and men escaped from Libby Prison in Richmond, Virginia, in 1864. The tunnel's starting-point inside the prison was behind a disused stove. It was necessary to remove and replace about seventy bricks each night while digging the tunnel. They dug until they estimated that the end of the tunnel was under a carriage shed across the street, then worked upwards. On the night of February 9, 1864, 109 men escaped. Few made their way back to Union lines, as most were quickly recaptured.[2]

Personal Safety

Digging a tunnel is a fairly safe method of escape. There's no danger of getting shot inside the tunnel. Theoretically, there was danger from collapsing tunnels, but actually, because of the care taken by the diggers, nobody was ever killed this way. This record is in sharp contrast to that of commercial mines, where managers are constantly prodding for more production, even at the cost of ignoring safety measures.

In certain cases, guards who have detected the tunnel have waited until the escapers tried to use it, and met them at the exit with dogs and guns. However, there were no escapers who resisted at this point, and the guards recaptured them without violence.

Tunnel Types

There are two types of tunnels. One is the well-planned and engineered tunnel, carefully dug, shored, and camouflaged, intended to serve more than one attempt. The other is the "mole," a quick and dirty tunnel dug near the surface and intended to last only one escape. The mole tunnel breaks all the rules, and is truly an opportunistic attempt.

The Tunnel Entrance

The most important aspect of organizing a tunnel escape is to choose a tunnel entrance hard to detect. Experience had shown that digging under a barrack, while very convenient, also made it easy for the guards to find the tunnel entrance. Although the POWs tried to disguise the entrances, often by fitting lids that were actually trays to hold layers of dirt several feet deep, the guards developed techniques of probing for entrances which soon revealed them. Therefore, the diggers made every effort to find novel and unusual locations for tunnel entrances.

Favorite locations were those that allowed clever disguising of the entrance. In German camps, POWs took advantage of the fastidious-ness of their captors, and some entrances began at the bottom of latrine ditches. Another entrance was in the middle of a washbasin which the prisoners left filled with dirty water. Yet another was under the floor bricks of a stove. A frame allowed swinging the entire stove and floor back to reveal the entry. Yet another began on the third floor of Colditz Castle. A fourth, used in the famous "Trojan Horse" escape (also referred to later as "Wooden Horse"), began in the middle of an athletic field.

The most convenient entrances were those already built. A man-hole cover was an obvious choice in one escape attempt from Colditz. The reason it was possible to use this was that the Germans felt that it was secure, as it was located inside the prisoners' canteen, locked at night. Prisoners made a passkey to gain access, and the work pro-ceeded from that point.[3]

Tools and Materials

Because POWs are often in a more liberal regime than criminal prisoners, they have more with which to work, including both tools and raw materials. In some cases, they don't have to improvise very much, as gardening implements can serve well to dig at a tunnel face. Bed boards and floorboards serve as tunnel shoring. Tin cans, from Red Cross parcels, made improvised air ducts.

Look-outs

The tunnel was most vulnerable while the entrance was open and work was proceeding. This was usually at the beginning of the tunnel, when there was not enough space underground to store the day's diggings and the workers had to bring it up as they dug. Once the tunnel had progressed beyond the vertical shaft and the initial alcove, it was only necessary to open the trap to allow entrance and exit from the tunnel. This was only a few minutes at a time, enough to allow the changing shifts to climb in and out, and to bring the rubble to the surface. It was necessary to choose the time carefully, and to post a screen of look-outs to warn of approaching guards. POWs invested much time and effort in their tunnels, and took other measures to safeguard them.

Additional Safeguards

One was to start several tunnels at once, depending on at least one remaining undetected until completion. In many cases, the discovered tunnels served as decoys. Another technique was to dig one tunnel underneath another. If the top tunnel fell to the guards, it would be possible to dig another shaft and continue with the lower tunnel.

At times, the search for the entrance could be quite extensive. Guards would evict the residents from a barrack under suspicion while they dismantled everything in it.

Digging

The difficulty of digging varied with the soil composition and the implements available. In light and sandy soil, upon which many German prison camps were built, working the tunnel face was relatively easy. By contrast, many American criminal prisons are built upon granite or other type of rock, making excavation almost impossible. Criminal prisoners also live under tighter security and more restrictions than do many POWs. Most are not allowed to keep knives and forks in their cells, because these are easy to convert into weapons or primitive digging implements.

Digging is also very time-consuming. Time worked against the POWs because each day increased the chances of detection. In most cases, the diggers had to come up to present themselves for the appel, or head count, and this meant that the tunnel entrance had to be closed and covered up against detection. This slowed the work, and gave the guards more opportunities to detect the entrance.

The water table can be important. In most camps, this was below the level of most tunnels, but at Barth, a German WWII POW camp, the ground flooded in wet weather, which impeded digging.[4]

In some cases, such as the three tunnels dug at the North Compound at Stalag Luft III, it was necessary to dig the tunnels very deeply. The Germans had buried microphones at six feet depth to detect digging, and the prisoners decided to dig their tunnels at a depth of 25 feet to overcome this.

Disposal of the Diggings

Transporting the rubble back from the digging face became more of a problem the longer the tunnel proceeded. At the outset, a cardboard Red Cross box was adequate. Later, the diggers placed the rubble into bags, metal trays, or boxes, which others dragged through the tunnel with ropes. Long tunnels required railways, as described below.

Disposing of the diggings was a problem from the start. This was especially difficult when the topsoil was of a different color than the sub-strata, which often was the case. Some tried to scatter the diggings around the prison yard. One way to do this was to use pants with ties in the cuffs. Prisoners would pour the dirt down inside their pants, then release it gradually by pulling the strings as they walked around the yard on exercise (Figure 7 on page 94).

Often, the subsoil would contrast with the topsoil and an alert guard would note this. Tower guards, because of the high viewpoints, would be the first to notice. When this happened, it was an unequivocal sign to the guards that a tunnel was in progress, and they would intensify their efforts to discover it.

Other ways to dispose of the diggings were to pour the soil down the latrine, use it in flower beds, or pour it into specially-prepared hides. When POWs disposed of the diggings in their gardens, they had to time it just right. Working a vegetable garden out of season would arouse suspicion.

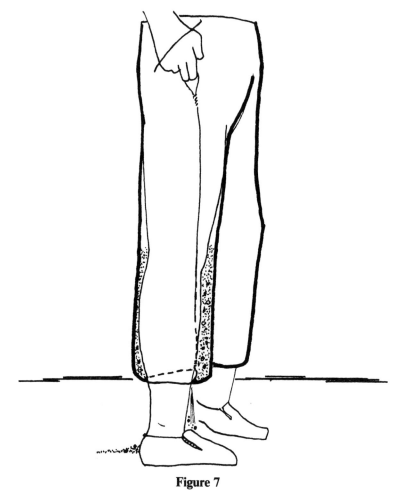

Figure 7

*Rigged pant legs allow for inconspicuous disposal
of dirt extracted from tunnels.*

In some cases, dug up soil went into hollow walls, or into hollow spaces within buildings. Disused airshafts and staircases were rare examples. In some cases, it went into the attic. This brought the danger of the ceiling's collapsing, which happened at least once. Even without a collapse, if any sand leaked through the cracks between the boards, it would give away the secret.

Another type of place suitable for disposing of diggings was any construction site within the compound. If there was a new latrine under construction, tunnel rubble would blend in easily with the excavated dirt from the septic tank. Any new building needed a foundation, and digging this would provide cover for disposing of tunnel dirt.

Tunnel Safety

Because prisoners could dig only in soft soil, lacking the tools to dig through rock, tunnels were prone to collapse. A system of shorings was necessary to keep the tunnels open. These usually were improvised from bed slats because these were a convenient source of wood. Each prisoner would be "assessed" one or two of his bed slats for the common effort. This points up how difficult it was to restrict knowledge of a tunnel in a POW camp.

There were a couple of near-misses at Stalag Luft III, with collapses of sand into the vertical shafts at the beginnings of two tunnels. Because the diggers were alert, and took precautions, they were not caught in the collapses, and were able to repair the damage quickly.

Providing fresh air to the digging crew was important, once the tunnel progressed beyond a few feet. The danger of asphyxiation was severe in some tunnels because the only light was from candles and improvised lamps. Prisoners sacrificed some of their cooking oils and fats to provide fuel for the lamps. A few tunnels had electricity, if the facilities permitted running a wire down the entrance. This was impossible, obviously, for the tunnel that began in the middle of an athletic field, as the "Trojan Horse" (or "Wooden Horse") tunnel did. In some cases, the diggers bored small holes to the surface, but this could give the tunnel away if the holes came out on bare ground within sight of the guards. Plumes of condensation coming up from the holes in the winter would mark the tunnel's location to anyone who cared to look and to think about what he saw.

To provide ventilation, prisoners improvised ducts from a series of food cans, emptied and with both top and bottom cut out, laid end to end. In some cases, it was necessary to solder the cans to each other to stop leaks. The duct would run from a point beyond the top of the shaft down to an alcove at the bottom of the vertical shaft. Because there was no room inside the shaft or tunnel for the duct, it was necessary to dig an additional tunnel at the side of the vertical shaft, behind the shoring, to house the duct. In the horizontal section of the tunnel, the air duct was usually in a cavity at one side or under the floor of the tunnel.

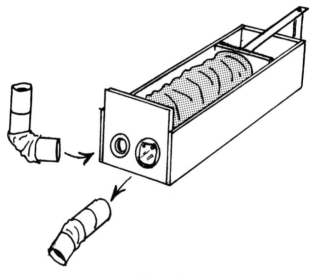

Figure 8

A bellows pump is improvised to provide fresh air to tunnelers.

A bellows pump served to propel air through the fresh air duct to the digging face. POWs improvised the pumps from army kit-bags.

A bag would be attached to a board with two large holes, each covered by a leather flap valve to ensure directional flow, as shown in Figure 8 on page 96.

The pump's intake would be the vertical pipe, and the exit hole would feed into the tunnel ductwork. The pump operator was a vital member of the digging crew, and he had to keep pumping as long as men were in the tunnel. The ducting would go as far as the tunnel face, to provide fresh air to the digger. The return flow would be back along the tunnel, with some air leaking out into the porous soil. An important point, in some tunnels, was exhausting the air. This usually carried the smell of heavy sweat, and could have attracted attention. Exhausting it through a stove's chimney was one way to avoid this.

A good design allowed bringing in fresh air even with the tunnel trap closed. This allowed work around the clock, if other factors were favorable. The air intake had to be disguised to avoid detection. One air intake was behind a perforated brick that was in the barrack's foundation.

Another feature necessary in some tunnels was a muffler to suppress the sound of the valve slaps. This was, in one case, a box lined with blankets and fitted with baffles.[5]

The digger would have to extend the ducting and the shoring as he progressed, to prevent the tunnel's collapse and to ensure his supply of fresh air. Using hand tools, a digger was able to progress at an average of a foot an hour.

When work was progressing, heating was not a problem. The layers of earth insulated from the cold, and the work itself produced heat. Diggers often wore light clothing, even in the winter. If work was held up because of a lighting failure, or because the system for evacuating rubble broke down, the chill could become a problem.

Travel

Travel within the tunnel was a major logistic problem. In short tunnels, diggers and escapees could simply crawl. Longer tunnels demanded more sophisticated transport. Ropes attached to wash basins served to haul dirt. The diggers dug alcoves to permit turning around in a tunnel. Without these turn-arounds, it would be necessary to crawl backwards for the entire length when returning to the vertical shaft because the tunnels were both low and narrow. Hardly any were as large as a yard square.

The longest tunnels had underground railways, consisting of small carts running on improvised narrow-gauge rails, usually made of wood. Rails were usually furring strips taken from barracks walls. The tunnel workers nailed the strips onto the floorboards, using a jig to keep the spacing between them constant. This made for a railway with a "gauge" of 12½″ in the railways at Stalag Luft III.[6]

The railway carts, or "trolleys," were also made of wood. Axles were of metal tubing with axle bearings improvised from hardwood. The wheels were wood with tin rimming, which served as tires and reduced wear.

The trolleys were used for transporting diggers to the tunnel face and back, but mostly for removing the rubble. The trolleys had ropes attached so that workers on each end could pull them through the tunnel.

The longest tunnels had transfer points, alcoves built into them, to allow traffic to pass. The alcoves were also used for storing materials, tools, and other supplies during the work. These also served as additional assembly points during the actual escape. In at least one tunnel, dug at Stalag Luft III, the alcoves were given the names of London subway stations.[7]

Sources

1. *Escape From Germany,* Aidan Crawley, NY, Simon and Schuster, 1956, pp. 17.

2. *The Master Book of Escapes,* Donald McCormick, NY, Franklin Watts, Inc., 1975, pp. 104-109.

3. *Colditz, The Full Story,* P. R. Reid, NY, St. Martin's Press, 1984, pp. 38-41.

4. *Escape From Germany,* pp. 151.
5. *Ibid.,* pp. 166.
6. *Ibid.,* pp. 166.
7. *Ibid.,* pp. 179.

Part III

11

Some Classic Escapes

There have been many ingenious plans for escape devised by both POWs and criminal escapers. Some plans were very simple. Others were so complex that they fell of their own weight.

Not all of the escapes described in this chapter succeeded. All were ingenious. All are worth telling for that reason.

The White Line in the Road

Two Allied soldiers escaped from their camp using a bucket of white paint and two brushes. They began by painting a white line down the center of the road that led through the main gate. When they arrived at the camp exit, they lit cigarettes and appeared to be goofing off. A guard told them to keep on working, and opened the inner gate so that they could get on with the job. When they reached the outer gate, another guard opened it to allow them to continue painting the line. They continued to paint the line until they were out of sight, and then took off.[1]

The Workman

In WWI, a certain Lieutenant Marcus Kaye of the Royal Flying Corps hid articles of civilian clothing, and a bag of metal scraps intended to simulate tools, inside the latrine. Just before shift change, he went into the latrine and changed his clothing, coming out dressed as a civilian and with his face and hands smeared with dirt, as a civilian laborer might look. He dismantled and inspected part of latrine's ventilation duct. When he had that section of it reassembled, he nodded to the guard to indicate that he had to climb the ladder to inspect the top section too. He then climbed the ladder out of the prison, inspected the pipe, and made his way down the hill to freedom.

Impersonating a Ferret

The roving inspectors known as "ferrets" were nuisances, but in one camp they inadvertently provided a means of escape. At Stalag Luft III, an RAF officer who spoke perfect German observed that, when the ferrets came in to inspect the camp at night, they unlocked the inner gate themselves, and identified themselves to the tower guards by shining their flashlights on the ground as they walked. They would then inspect where they wished, or go spend an hour in the kitchen. This behavior pattern suggested a way out.

The officer improvised a ferret uniform, which was only a jumpsuit, belt, and field service type cap. He also arranged for a POW with locksmithing skill to produce a master key to open the gate's padlock. He also obtained a flashlight by bribing a guard. He arranged for false papers, allowing him to travel inside Germany, and settled down to wait for the right moment.

One night, when the ferret was inside the compound, the escaper slipped out of his window and walked towards the inner gate, shining his flashlight upon the ground. He opened the gate with his key, but was unable to lock the padlock. He pushed it almost closed, and went towards the outer gate, where his false papers got him past the guard. He was several miles away from the camp when the genuine ferret found the open lock and gave the alert. A German patrol, aided by dogs, caught him at the Swiss frontier.[2]

Filling in the Ditch

Three POWs had escaped from Stalag Luft III through a mole tunnel, which had later collapsed, leaving a ditch which ran under the wire. Two British officers decided to impersonate German troopers assigned to fill in the ditch. They dressed in improvised German fatigue uniforms, and went up to the adjacent guard towers to inform the guards that they had been ordered to fill in the ditch. At this point, they noticed a real German approaching them with a spade. This German shouted to them, and they realized that their German language skill was not good enough to sustain a prolonged conversation. They picked up their sacks and tools and fled to the nearest washhouse, where they changed uniforms and hid their materials.

The Extra Germans

At Barth, a German POW camp, routine was for a party of German soldiers to enter the camp each evening to close the barrack shutters and lock the doors to enforce curfew. Two British officers decided to manufacture fake German uniforms, including rifles, and to join this party as they went back out the gate. This plan fell through when one of the genuine Germans started a conversation with one of the fakes. As the British officer could not hold up his end of the conversation, he was soon revealed. The other was discovered a few minutes later.

Colditz

The most notable German prison camp may have been Colditz, which was an establishment set up for incorrigible escapers and especially notable prisoners. The Germans gathered the hard-core escapers in one place in the hope that they'd be better able to keep an eye on them. They also calculated that Colditz Castle was escape-proof. Incredibly, they expected that, in view of the formidable obstacles, the POWs would give up any idea of escape. This turned out to be a very mistaken belief.

The huge Sagan camp, Stalag Luft III, held about 7,000 Allied personnel. Colditz, much smaller, held only about 800 at its peak. A guard company of about 280 men was enough to guard Sagan. Colditz often had as many guards as inmates. There were over 300 escape attempts from Colditz. Thirty of these were totally successful, with the escapers reaching their home countries.[3]

It's not too hard to explain why, as a maximum-security prison, Colditz was an almost total failure. By contrast to criminal prisons, concentration camps, and the austere Asian camps of WWI and later, Colditz was a country club. Prisoners received regular Red Cross parcels, had their own theater, were allowed civilian clothing to use as costumes in their theatrical productions, and generally were very well treated by the guards. There was no regime of starvation and constant beatings, as were typical in Asian prison camps, and there were regular visits by officials of the "protecting powers," such as Switzerland.

Discipline was very lax, by the standards of Southeast Asia. Prisoners were able to indulge in what they called "goon-baiting," a series of practical jokes upon the guards. One such was the dummy constructed out of straw, and let out of an upper-story window on a string. Guards seeing the dummy thought it was an escape attempt, and opened fire. The prisoners then let the dummy drop to the ground, but when guards approached they yanked it up into the air again.[4]

Another effort was to sabotage the pig swill. Leftovers from the camp rations normally were used as pig swill by the Germans, and some British POWs sabotaged it by pushing pieces of broken razor blades into rotten potatoes and other leftovers. The Germans noted the effects, and posted notices that they would severely punish anyone whom they caught committing such sabotage, but never did anything else. It's hard to imagine POWs in North Vietnam having any surplus food, rotten or not, to throw away, and it's harder yet to imagine the North Vietnamese viewing any such sabotage with good-natured tolerance.

The Wooden Horse

An RAF Lieutenant at Stalag Luft III thought of starting a tunnel where the guards would least expect it; in the middle of a playing field. The technique was to build a wooden vaulting horse which was large enough to carry two men, tools, and a cargo of rubble. The plan was to place the vaulting horse out on the playing field each day, and for the occupants to dig the tunnel while the horse was in use. The POWs would carry the horse in to the canteen before the afternoon appel. The main disadvantage of the technique was that it would be impossible to carry much dirt away each day, which would stretch the project out for months. The main advantage was that the tunnel's starting point was original and unlikely to be discovered. It was only necessary to put together a stout lid for the tunnel, one which would hold the weight of anyone walking on it and which would not ring with a hollow sound. For this reason the "lid" was set two feet down.

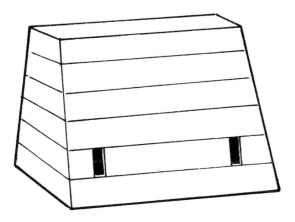

Figure 9

One novel approach to digging tunnels was this wooden vaulting horse. While men on the outside used it for recreation, men hidden on the inside dug tunnels.

The wooden horse is shown in Figure 9. Inside were several cross-beams to form seats and points from which to hang sacks of dirt. Slots in the horse allowed inserting long poles for carrying.

Although the idea appeared simple in principle, there were operational complications. The men who daily carried the horse in and out could not give any hint of the weight they were carrying, because the Germans knew that the hollow contraption was quite light. A POW, acting as "instructor," was stationed by the horse each minute that it was in use, to signal by means of taps when Germans were approaching.

The shaft was about eighteen inches square, to keep the volume of rubble minimal. This made for a very cramped tunnel. Ventilation was very poor because there was no fresh-air system, piping, or pump. The diggers pushed a narrow air hole through to the surface at one point, taking the risk of detection. There was concern that a German might notice condensation in the cold air, or that a guard dog might put a paw into the hole.

After the tunnel had progressed about forty feet it was necessary to work a two-man crew. One would dig while the other would drag the diggings back to the tunnel mouth, using a wash basin on a cord. Disposing of the dirt dug from the tunnel was a problem and a chore, but the POWs found solutions. They scattered dirt under the canteen and kitchen floors, and even in the canteen's roof. The gardens that some POWs had growing around the camp were receptacles for some dirt.

The Germans discovered the sand, but there were several other tunnels going simultaneously. German ferrets discovered some of these, which masked the existence of the wooden horse tunnel.

The tunnel eventually became just over 100 feet long, and the planned exit was in a ditch between a foot path and the road that ran beside the camp. This forced any escapee to cross the exposed width of the roadway to reach the woods, and suggested that a dark night would be best for the attempt. On the afternoon of the day planned, one escaper went down into the tunnel to get the exit ready. The POWs were able to keep the Germans from noticing his absence during the count. After the appel, POWs walked the horse out with three men in it. The plan was to have three escapees and one to close up the tunnel entrance, as they wanted to use the tunnel as many times as possible.

There had been slight miscalculation, and the exit was not as far out as they'd planned. Instead of being in the ditch, it cut the path on which the sentry walked. Nevertheless, the three escapers made for the woods and freedom. All three reached England, although the tunnel was no longer operational once the Germans discovered the exit.[5]

This escape was so remarkable that it became the subject of a book and a screen play after the war.

Mass Escapes

These usually don't work. Mass escapes make waves. In wartime Germany, any escape involving more than five persons had to be reported immediately to the high command. This caused a large-scale alert across the Reich, which cut the chances of successful evasion. Another point to consider is that most of the escapers are not skilled at evading recapture.

At Stalag IIIE, POWs dug a tunnel that was 227 feet long, and which led 52 men to freedom beyond the wire. This tunnel started under the floor of one of the barracks, and the prisoners were able to disperse the sand dug up in blind spots that the Germans could not see when they inspected the crawlways.

This tunnel took from January to May, 1942, to complete, but when it was finished the mass break rousted the Reich. The German High Command ordered troops, aircraft, and para-military groups such as Home Guard and Hitler Youth into the search. All escapees found themselves captive again within ten days.[6]

Oflag VIB was the scene of another mass escape, this one planned to go over the wire instead of under it. The camp's perimeter followed the standard pattern, with inner and outer fences. There were guard towers and searchlights to illuminate the fence at night. Two officers who were ardent escapers studied the problem, and realized that, if it were possible to put out the camp's lights upon demand, there would be a very good chance of rushing the fence and getting some men up and over the wire unseen.

As luck had it, the main fuse box for the camp's lights was inside the camp, accessible to the prisoners. They ran a test to see if it were possible to extinguish all of the camp's lights upon demand. The test proved successful, and planning for the escape began in earnest. The POWs designed a special two-part scaling ladder with a hinged upper section that would flop over and bridge the two fences. To work out the bugs, provide the men practice, and test how long the process would take, the escapers built a test facility in a barrack. This consisted of two wires ten feet off the floor to simulate the tops of the two fences. Testing showed that ten men with packs could set up the ladder and get over it in under a minute.

Based on these tests, the escape committee decided that the project would go on the night of August 30, 1942. That afternoon, prisoners built three more ladders. At the moment that the guards were on the extreme ends of their beats, prisoners fused the lighting circuits and the searchlights went out. The four teams rushed the fence and put their ladders over. Twenty-nine got over the wire. Of these, seventeen got beyond the immediate area of the camp without capture. Three officers made it all the way to England, the rest being recaptured within a few days.[7]

Another mass escape took place from Oflag XXIB, at Schubin. The prisoners started a tunnel in a latrine, using the septic tank itself to dispose of most of the dirt. They scattered the rest on paths around the camp, as it was winter and they were able to convince the guards that the dirt was to make the ice less slippery. When spring came, more dirt went into the vegetable gardens the prisoners tended.

The tunnel itself was almost luxurious by WWII standards. It was shored through all its length with boards and was two and a half feet square in section, which gave ample room for crawling comfortably. There was an anteroom between the latrine and the tunnel, which gave room to work or to wait during the escape attempt. D-Day was to be March 5, 1943. That evening, all thirty-two who were scheduled to go went into the tunnel or the ante-room.

The exit was five yards beyond the wire, in the inky blackness outside the light of the camp. Officers emerging from the tunnel could see the guards clearly, and were surprised that they themselves remained invisible.

When daylight came, the Germans were still unaware of the mass escape. Another officer, encouraged by what he saw, decided to take the chance of emerging from the tunnel exit in broad daylight. He changed into civilian clothing and went into the tunnel. He came out of the exit, the Germans still unaware, and walked off down the road.

At the morning appel, the security officer noticed the missing men and sounded the alarm. None of the escapers reached England, but not all were recaptured. Two drowned while trying to cross to Sweden.[8]

Another mass escape, using bluff and impersonation of German guards, took place at Stalag Luft III. This camp was divided into several compounds. In the North Compound, officers organized a clever ruse to get a large party of escapees out the gate. This depended on the German attention to personal hygiene.

Officers "discovered" lice in the compound, and notified the German command. The German administrators arranged for parties of POWs to be escorted out the gate and right along the road to another compound which contained the prison hospital. This was where the delousing station was located. Thick woods were on the other side of this road, and beyond the woods were the railway line and train station. The plan was to send two fake German guards to escort a party out of the gate. They would never reach the hospital, but would melt into the woods alongside the road.

To cover this getaway, which would be within sight of several watch-towers, it was necessary to capture the guards' attention. For this, the officers set up a second party, escorted by one fake guard. Their purpose would be not to escape, but to engage the attention of the guards within sight of the escaping party.

It was necessary to manufacture fake German uniforms and weapons to pull the masquerade off successfully. The uniforms were restyled RAF uniforms, and the pistol holsters were the genuine articles this time, secured by clandestine purchase from the Germans.

The three officers posing as German guards were fluent in the language.

At the appointed time, the prisoners scheduled for the fake delousing party assembled at the gate, and lined up for the "count" by the two fake guards. The timing was such that the gate guards had just come on duty, and were therefore unaware that the two fake guards had originated from inside the compound. The second party assembled behind the first. At the gate to the inner fence, the front guard showed the gate guard his forged pass, copied from a genuine one, and this got them through. The guard at the outer gate had seen the party pass the inner gate, and did not stop them as they went through. Twenty-nine POWs therefore were safely out the gate.

The second party now began. At the second gate, the guard stopped them and asked the fake German guard to step into the guardroom. The gate guard was suspicious and telephoned to check on the bona fides of the second party. He quickly discovered that it was a fake, and during the excitement the members of the first party dispersed into the woods. The camp security officer came to the guardroom, and confronted the members of the second party, admonishing them that escape was impossible because of the rigorous security measures. Meanwhile, one of the guards on duty telephoned to check whether or not the first party had arrived at the other compound. This disclosed that the party was fake, and the alarm went out. All of the escapers were caught, most in the area around the camp or railway station. One almost made it to the Swiss frontier.[9]

Harry

This was the code name of the tunnel used by POWs in the North Compound of Stalag Luft III for their escape on the night of March 23/24, 1944. This was the mass escape that led to the shooting-upon-recapture order.

There had been three tunnels, "Tom," "Dick," and "Harry," started in the spring of 1943. The Germans discovered "Tom," and there was no time to complete "Dick." The main effort, therefore, went into "Harry." This tunnel was 336 feet long, and came out beyond the wire, near a patrol path. It was a prodigious effort, having engaged a total of about 600 men during various phases of the project. The tunnel was completed on March 14, 1944, but the escape committee did not use it right away. Instead, they made an effort to plan the escape with as much thoroughness as they had the construction. This was where things began to go wrong.

By this time, there had been enough experience with mass escapes to show that they offered very poor chances of success in the percentage of escapees who made "home runs," escapes all the way to England. Part of the reason was quality. With many escapers let loose at one time, it was obvious that not all of them would be equally skilled in speaking German, and have the same knowledge of escape and evasion techniques. More importantly, a mass escape inevitably provoked a maximum effort from the Germans, and the entire Reich would be seeking the escapers. This was excellent reason for rationing use of the tunnel, letting out only a few well-prepared men each week, but the escape committee's judgment faltered on this point. Otherwise, the preparations were elaborate.

The reasons for choosing the night of March 23rd were that it would be a moonless night, and also a Friday night, with trains running on Saturday. Fewer trains ran on Sunday.

With about 600 candidates, the selection process was complex. The escape committee calculated that it would be possible to send off about 200 men during the eight dark hours. Logically, the first thirty places were for those who, because of language fluency or other reasons, had the best chance. They had to go first to catch the trains, which became infrequent after midnight. The next twenty places were for key escape organizers. Thirty key tunnel workers came next, and the last twenty were also important in the escape organization. Another hundred names came through drawing from a hat. To help ensure success, it was necessary to insert an experienced tunnel worker at each twentieth place in the list. Having people familiar with the tunnel and the operation of the railway system was vital to avoid problems.

All of the escapers had to prepare, and those without tunnel experience needed to be briefed on the procedures to follow. More, it was necessary to issue escape food and forged papers to all who were going. All had to pass an inspection, to ensure that they were not carrying too much clothing or gear to pass easily through the tunnel. Strict discipline in this regard was vital, because blocking the tunnel would impair the chances of everyone caught behind the jam.

It was also necessary to plan the way in which those selected would reach the barrack with the tunnel entrance. Guards were always alert to movements inside the camp, and a line of men entering a particular barrack, with none leaving, might attract attention. This measure was so successful that the guards, after the escape, thought that another tunnel from a nearby barrack existed.[10]

It was necessary to prepare the tunnel for the volume of traffic. Workers procured stout rope to put on the trolleys, in anticipation of heavy-duty use. They also laid strips of blankets on the rails near the entrance and exit to muffle the sound of the wheels. They also installed extra light bulbs to illuminate the tunnel better, for the benefit of those who had never been inside. They also hung "blackout" blankets to prevent light leakage from alerting the Germans.

At the exit, two tunnel engineers were to make the break to the surface, and then control traffic out of the tunnel. One traffic controller would lie beside the hole, facing the camp, and control the timing. Another stretched a rope to a tree at the edge of the woods, to guide those emerging from the tunnel. The escape committee devised different routes out of the woods for different groups of escapees.

Although the plan had been to start at 9:30 P.M. there were delays, and it was not until after 10 P. M. that the exit was open. The first man at the bottom of the entrance shaft moved out at 10:30. Then the problems began. The third man's suitcase, despite briefings and inspections, was too large. It was necessary to send it on a separate trolley. Other difficulties slowed the rate of travel and the number out.

At a quarter to midnight, an air raid caused the Germans to cut the power to the camp, to assure that no lights showed. This blacked out the tunnel, and it took several minutes to deploy the emergency lights, margarine lamps. However, the blackout also knocked out the tower lights and searchlights, which helped the escapers.

Other problems came up, mostly caused by the escapers themselves. Most centered around trying to carry too much, either excessively fat blanket rolls, or too much escape gear packed into the clothing. Despite drastic measures, such as forbidding any more blanket rolls, progress did not improve. An accident resulted in two frames knocked out of place, and a partial collapse of the tunnel. This caused a fifty-minute delay until workers were able to repair it and restore service.

More men went through until 4:55 A. M. A passing guard turned and saw a shadow alongside the tunnel entrance. He raised his rifle, and a man who had been hiding behind a nearby tree came out, imploring the German not to shoot. The German was so startled that his finger jerked the trigger, and the shot went off, fortunately going wild. This, however, roused the security forces and the jig was up. Some of the men came scurrying back along the tunnel, saying that the Germans were right behind them.

Seventy-six men had gotten through the tunnel. The German high command simply "went ape" and there were severe reprisals. Of the 76, only three reached England. The rest wound up prisoners again. Fifty of these were shot by the Gestapo. The Germans dispersed the rest among several concentration camps and POW camps.

It became clear that mass escape led mainly to disasters. Most involved never made it home. About 80 years before, the escape of 109 Union officers and men from Libby Prison, in Richmond, Virginia, resulted in most being recaptured. It's unfortunate that writers continue to glorify mass escapes, because such accounts can lead to more in the future, and reduce the chances of success of smaller escapes.

General Henri Giraud

Henri Giraud was a French military officer who had fought in both WWI and WWII. In WWI, he was wounded and captured by the Germans, but escaped from prison camp despite his injury. In WWII, he had attained the rank of General, and the Germans again captured him during the assault of 1940. They imprisoned him in Konigstein, which was on a 150-foot cliff, and where Giraud began to plan his escape. The first step was to improve his rusty German, so that he could pass for a native once outside. For this project, he got the active cooperation of his guards, who didn't realize his real reason for polishing his skill in their language.

He also made a copy of a map of the area, to guide him after his exit. Packages from home were tied with string, which he saved and wove into a rope. One of his prisoner colleagues was scheduled to be sent home because of the severity of his wounds, and Giraud sent a code with him, to be delivered to his wife. He used this channel of communication to arrange the details of his escape. One of the first requests he made was for some wire to reinforce his improvised rope. This came to him inside a ham sent from home. He got other escape items sent to him, concealed within food packages, and made arrangements for help once he got outside the walls.

The Allies were seeking another noted person to represent Free France, as relations with de Gaulle were often stormy. The Allied secret services arranged for an agent to meet Giraud outside the walls and provide him with clothing, false papers, and money. He made his way to Switzerland, then France, and finally a British submarine met him on the coast and evacuated him to North Africa.[11]

Von Werra

Captain Franz Von Werra was a Luftwaffe fighter pilot shot down over England in September, 1940. He twice escaped from prison camps in Britain, and on one occasion almost managed to steal a Hurricane and fly back to Germany with it. At the last moment, an alert RAF officer put a pistol to his head and ordered him out of the cockpit.

He was sent across to Canada in early 1941, and during the train ride to the prison camp, jumped out of a lavatory window. This was during winter, and he was able to walk across the frozen Saint Lawrence River to the United States, which was not yet in the war. Police in Plattsburgh, New York, arrested him for vagrancy and illegal entry, but the German Consul in New York had Von Werra released to his custody. Although the Canadian Government had asked for Von Werra's extradition, before this could take place the consul helped him smuggle himself out of the United States to South America. The next leg of the trip was by neutral ship to Africa, then to Spain, and finally repatriation to Germany. Von Werra was later killed on the Russian Front.[12]

Escape by Air

Two other German pilots, Lieutenants Schnable and Wappler, sneaked onto an RAF base and made off with a training aircraft. Unfortunately, they ran out of fuel near the coast and had to land at another RAF base, where they posed as Dutch officers. They were offered hospitality, dinner and housing, and planned to continue their interrupted flight in the morning. However, the news of their escape had by then circulated, and they were re-arrested and taken back to camp the next day.[13]

In early 1941, three Canadian pilots, Flying Officers Donaldson, Thom, and Flynn, escaped from a prison fort at Thorn, in Poland. After making good their escape, they reached a German air base in Poland wearing home-made German fatigue uniforms. There they commandeered an aircraft and tried to start it to fly to Sweden, but failed. The control tower officials had noticed their performance and sent a Luftwaffe under-officer, who soon found out that they did not speak German. The jig was up. As punishment and precaution, all three wound up in Colditz.[14]

A successful attempt by British airmen occurred during a flight from Greece to Italy. They were being flown to a prison camp in Italy when they hijacked the Italian flying boat and diverted it to Malta.[15]

There have been very few escapes using the helicopter, which is superbly suited for the task. The main reason is the scarcity of helicopters, which makes it very easy to trace one used in an attempt. However, when there is an attempt, it's usually successful.

In August, 1971, Joel Kaplan and Carlos Castro escaped by helicopter from a Mexican prison. There was a short flight to a nearby airfield, and a quick transfer to a waiting fixed-wing aircraft which took them out of the country.

The Irish Republican Army set up a spectacular helicopter escape for three of its leaders in 1973. Seamus Towmey, Kevin Mallon, an Joe O'Hagen were incarcerated in Mountjoy Prison in Dublin. A man with an American accent, who called himself "Mr. Leonard," chartered an Alouette helicopter from a local firm. His purported reason was to do some aerial photography of country estates. Leonard directed the pilot to land at a specified site, where armed and masked men surrounded the craft. They instructed the pilot to fly to the prison, land in the yard, and pick up the escapees, who were exercising. They then flew to another spot, where the prisoners transferred to automobiles.[16]

The Glider

Starting in the spring of 1944, POWs in Colditz built a catapult-launched glider in the attic of one of the castle's wings. The work took place in a section of the attic walled off from the rest, with the partition disguised to look like the end wall. The two-man glider was to be of wood, with cotton fabric and dope made from millett.[17]

The glider was a high-wing design, with a nose piece of molded "papier-mache," and the wings supported by triangulated front and rear spar struts. The launching was to be down a track made of wooden saddles made to fit on the peaked roof. Power for the launch was to be a rope, quick-release device, and a bathtub full of concrete dropped down sixty feet through several holes in floors. A suitable pasture a couple of hundreds of yards from the castle was to be the landing ground. The designers calculated that the glider would, upon launching, leave its 60-foot ramp at about 27 miles per hour. From this height and speed, it would be possible to glide about 900 feet.[18]

The plan was to launch at night, to avoid the assembly of the catapult track and glider being seen by the Germans. Understandably, there could be no test flight. As it happened, the war ended before the plan was ready, and the glider never flew. Nobody can say for sure that it would have been airworthy.

Criminal Escapes

By far, criminal escapes are not structural escapes. The most common type is not returning from work-release assignments, or "walk-aways" by trustees. However, there have been some structural escapes worth noting. Some of these show ingenuity. Others show incredible stupidity or complacency by the guards.

The Befford Escape

Befford was a defendant being taken up in an elevator for trial in the Pima County Courthouse, Tucson, Arizona. He snatched the pistol from the deputy who was guarding him, shut the deputy up in the elevator cage, and made his way out of the building before the alarm went out. Officials sealed the building and conducted a room by room search before concluding that Befford had gotten away from them. This gave Befford several hours' head start.

The Escape From the Van

Prisoners in front of a local courthouse kicked out the windows of a Sheriff's van in Tempe, Arizona, and made their escape.

The False Ceiling

A prisoner in a main sheriff's jail in Maricopa County, Arizona, realized that the false ceiling gave him a chance to get to the unsecured part of the building unseen. He removed a ceiling panel and climbed up into the false ceiling space and crawled to freedom, letting himself down in an outer office from which he was able to walk out the door. In other cases, prisoners were able to pick up guards' keys and let themselves out.[19]

A criminal prison inmate made a papier-mache replica of a small auto pistol. The handgun was about the size of a .25 caliber Browning, with a bright metal insert at the ejection port to simulate a barrel breech. The inmate arranged to be transported to a nearby hospital, claiming a medical problem. When he and the armed detention officer arrived in the hospital parking lot, the prisoner produced his fake gun and disarmed the officer. Armed with the officer's revolver, he made good his escape, leaving the fake behind.[20]

No Limits

The cliche, "the sky's the limit," would ordinarily apply to prison escapes, except that we've seen that there truly is no limit. Prisoners will literally take to the sky to escape. In the future, we may see even more imaginative techniques of escape, to offset increasingly effective and oppressive security measures.

Sources

1. *Prisoners Of War,* A. J. Barker, NY, Universe Books, 1975, p. 152.

2. *Escape From Germany,* Aidan Crawley, NY, Simon and Schuster, 1956, pp. 67-69.

3. *Colditz: The Great Escapes,* Ron Baybutt, Boston, Little, Brown, And Company, 1982, pp. 8-9.

4. *Escape from Colditz, (The Colditz Story),* P. R. Reid, NY, Berkley Books, 1952, p. 141.

5. *Escape From Germany,* pp. 75-79.

6. *Ibid.,* pp. 123-126.

7. *Ibid.,* pp. 126-130.

8. *Ibid.,* pp. 135-141.

9. *Ibid.,* pp. 141-147.

10. *Ibid.,* p. 186.

11. *The Master Book of Escapes,* Donald McCormick, NY, Franklin Watts, Inc., 1975, pp. 40-47.

12. *Prisoners of War,* Ronald H. Bailey, Chicago, IL, Time-Life Books, 1981, p. 69.

13. *Prisoners Of War,* A. J. Barker, p. 161.

14. *They Have Their Exits,* Airey Neave, London, Coronet Books, 1953, p. 28.

15. *Prisoners Of War,* A. J. Barker, p. 161.

16. *The Master Book of Escapes,* pp. 143-144.

17. *Colditz, The Full Story,* P. R. Reid, NY, St. Martin's Press, 1984, pp. 265-266.

18. *Colditz: The Great Escapes,* pp. 124-125.

19. *Police Product News,* January, 1986, pp. 36-39.

20. *Improvised Weapons in American Prisons,* Jack Luger, Port Townsend, WA, Loompanics Unlimited, 1985, p. 59.

Part IV

12

If You're Captured

From reading these accounts of life in confinement, and descriptions of both security and escape methods, you can easily see some important points to follow in case you're ever in a similar situation. These will help both your immediate circumstances and your chances of attaining early release. In reviewing these points, you'll note the remarkable similarity to the rules for survival in case of being taken hostage.

Captivity

- The first and most important point is that TIME IS NOT ON YOUR SIDE! The first moments of captivity provide the best opportunities to get away. Often, all that stands between you and freedom is the alertness of your captors, who are combat soldiers and not experienced guards. If they don't execute you on the spot, you have a good chance of evasion.

- If you're transported to a prison building or camp, you'll have bars, walls, and barbed wire between you and freedom. You may be the victim of a rough interrogation, which may include physical torture. This will leave you fatigued and possibly with physical injuries. Your physical condition will deteriorate with time, as prison diets are usually poor. Your morale will suffer, the intended result of the malnutrition.

- If you're injured or ill, don't expect speedy medical treatment. On the contrary, medical attention may well be a bargaining chip used by your captors during interrogation. On March 24, 1985, U.S. Army Major Arthur Nicholson was shot by Soviet troopers and refused medical help because he did not sign a confession exonerating the Soviets from responsibility for shooting him.[1]

- Throughout history, disease has caused more casualties among fighting men than enemy action. This is especially true in the primitive and often unsanitary conditions of a prison camp. In the tropics, disease is an especially severe threat.

- You may, in any event, be slated for a quick execution shortly after capture. Some combatants just don't take prisoners. Others are too short on food and resources to house POWs. If you're a downed flier, you may be mobbed by civilians who have been bombed and who want to take it out on you.

- Don't be surprised if you're treated as a criminal instead of a POW. If you're fighting in a civil war, your captors may not have signed the Geneva Convention, or may not recognize it. If you're a flier, even though you're part of the regular armed forces, you may be accused of war crimes, such as bombing civilians, and denied POW status.

- Don't make yourself conspicuous. If your objective is to escape, or just to live through your term of imprisonment, attracting attention from either guards or other inmates is undesirable. It's especially important not to give anyone the impression that you've got something they want, such as information.

- Keep to yourself. While you don't want to get the reputation of being anti-social or a hermit, you also don't want to reveal too much about yourself to others. If you're posing as an officer, revealing too much might expose you. Otherwise, you might be talking to a snitch. If you have important secret information, of course, you need to avoid revealing it and revealing that you have it.

If You're a Member of the Armed Forces

- Give only your name, rank, and serial number to your captors at first. Keep in mind that you may be interrogated and/or tortured, and that your government does not expect you to resist torture indefinitely. You must, however, put up a show of resistance.

- If you're a member of the armed forces, never give your "parole," your promise not to escape, or sign any document to that effect. Several countries, including the United States, forbid their servicemen to give parole. If you ever escape after giving your captor your parole, he'll be very angry if you're recaptured. You may also find that you've given up your POW status by signing the document, and that your captor will punish you severely as a criminal.

- Keep in mind that, if you talk more than the minimum with your captor, you may be charged with treason after repatriation, especially if you develop enemies among your fellow prisoners. Some people will lie to settle old scores. Defending yourself against this charge will be easier if you have scars on your body, or some broken bones.

- Give yourself a promotion. If you're an enlisted man, "promote" yourself to Lieutenant or Captain. There are enough of these in most armies to ensure that they don't all know each other. You'll probably get away with the impersonation for the duration. Lying to the enemy is not a crime.

Being an officer gets you extra privileges, such as an officer's camp. Like it or not, the class system is still with us, even in the armed forces of the "Western Democracies." The officers get the best; enlisted men get the rest, even in captivity.

Be aware that officers have their problems, too. Your captor may conclude that, as an officer, you must have vital information denied to enlisted men. If so, you may be in for some rigorous interrogation.

If you're captured by Asian Communists, the odds are that you'll get extra bad treatment as an officer, following their objective to break down class differences. You probably will be tortured for the information you presumably have.

If You're a Free-Lancer

- You may be involved in an irregular activity, such as a mercenary action or a civil war. If so, expect to be branded as a "terrorist" and criminal. You'll be in the hands of the security police, who will see you as an object, not a person. This means that they'll try to use you to get information on others in your movement, try to "turn" you as an informer or double agent, or use you to bait a trap for others on your side. You may also wind up as the accused in a "show trial," in which the verdict will be pre-determined despite the appearance of a legal process. All this makes it clear that the best course is to decide not to be captured.

Interrogation

- Be wary of questionnaires and "Red Cross" forms. These are almost always bogus.

- Also be wary of enemy officers and/or interrogators who try to become friendly with you and question you about your home. The odds are that they're just trying to get you used to speaking with them, and will gradually lead the conversation around to what they want to know.

- Expect endless questioning and other psychological techniques, which can include totally false accusations. You can spend hours defending yourself against these, but this will be to wear down your resistance, and to render you more vulnerable.

- Sooner or later you'll be offered a "deal," in which you have the opportunity to sign a confession, or to provide information, in return for better treatment, medical attention, or even your freedom. If you're injured, you can be terribly vulnerable to this type of offer.

Informers

- Also remember that some of your fellow POWs may be informers. There's usually at least one in every camp. Don't make accusations unless you're absolutely sure, though, because if true, they might lead to your death warrant. If false, you will be doing your suspect a great injustice. If you suspect someone of informing, report this to your superior officer or the camp committee. Be prepared to give clear reasons to support your suspicions.

- Because one or more of your fellow POWs might be a snitch, don't discuss sensitive topics with anyone who doesn't "need to know." Some fellow POWs need to know about escape attempts, but nobody in the camp needs to know details of any classified missions you may have had before being captured.

Rescue

- Don't sit around waiting for your side to rescue you. There were some brilliant attempted rescues of POWs in WWII, as in the Hammelberg Raid, but this eventually failed.[2] However, during the Korean War nobody even tried. By the time of the Vietnam Era the U.S. Armed forces had become unable to pull it off at all. The Son Tay Raid is an example. When it took place the POW camp had been vacant for months.

- Although your government will have enjoined you to keep faith with it, the really important point is to keep faith with yourself and your family. Don't think that your safety and best interests count for very much with your government. You are expendable, as are all military men.

- The approach of the war's end may result in your camp being evacuated, with guards marching the prisoners away from the advancing front. On the road, you may be strafed by friendly aircraft.

- Finally, be aware that the end of the war may bring about your liberation, but may also result in your being killed in reprisal. If the war ends with a negotiated peace, POWs may easily become bargaining counters in the discussions. That could postpone your release for a couple of years.

Sources

1. *United Press International,* June 20, 1988.

2. *Prisoners of War,* Ronald H. Bailey, Chicago, IL, Time-Life Books, 1981, pp. 174-176.

For Further Reading

There have been many books dealing with prisons, POW camps, escape methods, and prison survival published. A few of the more useful ones are listed here:

Colditz, The Full Story, P. R. Reid, NY, St. Martin's Press, 1984. This is a revised version of the author's previous Colditz book, listed below. It provides a much fuller account because of the author's access to diaries and other accounts by the people who were there.

Colditz: The Great Escapes, Ron Baybutt, Boston, Little, Brown, And Company, 1982. This is truly the "picture book" of Colditz escapes and escapers. A German photographer took most of the photographs illustrating this volume, showing the actual people involved at the time they were imprisoned in Colditz. The photographs also show many tunnels, trap doors, escape tools, fake uniforms, and other contemporary items. Also included is a photograph of the glider constructed secretly in the attic.

Escape From Colditz, P. R. Reid, NY, Berkley Publishing Corp., 1952. This is a personal account by a British Army Officer who escaped from Colditz during WWII.

Escape From Germany, Aidan Crawley, NY, Simon and Schuster, 1956. This is a very complete account of British escapes from various prison camps in Germany. The author lists many techniques that worked well for the escapees, who often had to improvise their tools and equipment. This is probably the most instructive book to read for a cataloging of escape techniques. The volume was classified for ten years because the descriptions of British escape techniques might prove valuable to a potential enemy.

Evasion And Escape, Field Manual 21-77, Washington, DC, Headquarters, Department of the Army, 1958. This is an older, unclassified version of the standard army text on the subject. Its main strength is that it provides some basic information for an American who may become a POW. It covers enemy interrogation techniques, and induced confessions. The main weakness is that it is too full of ideology, with not enough practical information on how to survive in a POW camp or escape from one.

Improvised Weapons in American Prisons, Jack Luger, Port Townsend, WA, Loompanics Unlimited, 1985. This book has many photographs showing improvised weapons that prison inmates produce. It also offers commentary on conditions in criminal prisons.

Hacksaw, Edward R. Jones, NY, Donald I. Fine, Inc., 1988. This is a personal account by a convicted felon who acquired a strong reputation as an escaper. The main value of this volume is that it provides a candid view of the mind-sets and weaknesses of lawmen and prison officials.

The Hate Factory, W. G. Strong, Agoura, CA, Paisano Publications, 1982. This is a graphic account of the 1980 riot at the New Mexico State Penitentiary and the conditions leading up to it. The descriptions of the prison officials give a good impression of the mentality in civilian prison administrations.

The Master Book of Escapes, Donald McCormick, NY, Franklin Watts, Inc., 1975. This is an interesting, well-illustrated popularization that's worth reading for entertainment. It also contains some valuable information on methods of escape.

Prisoners of War, Ronald H. Bailey, Chicago, IL, Time-Life Books, 1981. This is part of a series on World War II, and is well-illustrated and surprisingly complete and well-researched for a popular publication. The author went to a lot of trouble to gather statistics and make comparisons between the prospects faced by POWs in various theaters of war. Particularly interesting is the very good treatment given to German and Italian POWs in camps in the continental United States. The POWs found it hard to believe, at first, that they were being better fed than in their own countries.

Prisoners of War, A. J. Barker, NY, Universe Books, 1975. This is an overview of the history of prisoners of war, from primitive times to the modern era of the Geneva Convention.

The Raid, Benjamin F. Schemmer, NY, Avon Books, 1976. This book, although mainly a description and glorification of the unsuccessful Son Tay raid, contains as a sidelight some valuable information on prison camps in Southeast Asia. The accounts of daily life among the POWs shows the contrast between the "country club" German camps of WWII and the hostile environment of Vietnam.

They Have Their Exits, Airey Neave, London, Coronet Books, 1953. This is a personal account by a British Army Officer who was taken prisoner in 1940 and confined in Colditz. He and a Dutch Officer were the first to escape from Colditz in 1942. Neave went on to work for MI-9, the British escape organization, arranging escape lines and communication with men inside the wire.

Index

YOU WILL ALSO WANT TO READ: